Investing for Beginners

Stock Market Investing, Mutual Fund Investing, Commodities Investing

(Learn Forex, Options Trading, Futures and Real Estate)

David Walters

Published By **Bella Frost**

David Walters

All Rights Reserved

Investing for Beginners: Stock Market Investing, Mutual Fund Investing, Commodities Investing (Learn Forex, Options Trading, Futures and Real Estate)

ISBN 978-1-77485-635-2

All rights reserved. No part of this guidebook shall be reproduced in any form without permission in writing from the publisher except in the case of brief quotations embodied in critical articles or reviews.

Legal & Disclaimer

The information contained in this ebook is not designed to replace or take the place of any form of medicine or professional medical advice. The information in this ebook has been provided for educational & entertainment purposes only.

The information contained in this book has been compiled from sources deemed reliable, and it is accurate to the best of the Author's knowledge; however, the Author cannot guarantee its accuracy and validity and cannot be held liable for any errors or omissions. Changes are periodically made to this book. You must consult your doctor or get professional medical advice before using any of the suggested remedies, techniques, or information in this book.

Upon using the information contained in this book, you agree to hold harmless the Author from and against any damages, costs, and expenses, including any legal fees potentially resulting from the application of any of the information provided by this guide. This disclaimer applies to any damages or injury caused by the use and application, whether directly or indirectly, of any advice or information presented, whether for breach of contract, tort, negligence, personal injury, criminal intent, or under any other cause of action.

You agree to accept all risks of using the information presented inside this book. You need to consult a professional medical practitioner in order to ensure you are both able and healthy enough to participate in this program.

Table of contents

Chapter 1: The Basics Of Investing _1

Chapter 2: Make A Sense Of Yourself _____ 16

Chapter 3: Are You Interested In Pursuing A Career? _____ 45

Chapter 4: Be Aware Of Your Money Habits _____ 56

Chapter 5: Tips To Guard Yourself From Fraud When You Invest ____ 68

Chapter 6: What Financial Investment Important For You? __75

Chapter 7: The Kinds Of Index Funds _____ 93

Chapter 8: Setting Your Financial Goal _____ 110

Chapter 9: Conversion Of Currency _____ 117

Chapter 10: Mutual Fund Categories/Asset Class _____ 123

Chapter 11: Should I Be A Swing Trader? _____131

Chapter 12: 7 Top Real Estate Investing Jobs _____147

Chapter 13: Evictions _____166

Conclusion _____178

Chapter 1: The Basics of investing

Looking into investment options

The investment world is vast and filled with many possibilities and opportunities. One of the most appealing aspects about investing is that there's something for anyone. If you're just starting out or have been investing for a long time with short- or long-term goals, or just need to try something new there is bound to be something that's right for you. But, it's important to realize that this isn't a make wealthy quick scheme that promises you are likely to be able to earn millions in a matter of hours. It is first necessary to be aware of its various aspects, establish objectives, and then choose the type of investment you'd like to make in. To be successful in the investing world is a matter of perseverance, commitment and an knowledge of the various aspects. This chapter will include a comprehensive description of the various types of financial instruments, including their pros and drawbacks, along with the steps needed to be successful in investing in them.

Stocks & Bonds

Bonds and stocks are two crucial building blocks for investing. Stocks are ownership rights directly in businesses , whereas bond are loans. Many products related to stock and bonds have been developed in the last few years, like Mutual funds as well as default swaps. These investments are fantastic but it is the responsibility to know which options will help you achieve your financial objectives. When you purchase stock, you'll take the ownership of a specific company. One of the advantages of ownership direct is that the process can be completed quite simple, and there aren't any management fees or other persons that are involved. The cost of purchasing individual stocks is reasonable often, it may cost just $10 or less. One disadvantage is that you need to be aware of how the investments are performing every day. That's why you should at a minimum, an knowledge of accounting concepts and be up to date with reports from companies. Bonds are likely to lend money to entities like individuals, businesses or government. It's the same as buying cars: you have to bargain to obtain the best price. The bond you purchase needs to be aware of the rights you are entitled to the company's assets in case bankruptcy occurs.

The market's fluctuations could affect the stock market and other markets.

The Dow Jones is believed to be one of the largest financial markets. Everyday, traders engage in five trillion dollars worth of trades. Because of Dow Jones being an international market, the events that occur throughout the world can impact instantly on the value of currencies and exchange rates. This article will describe the effect from global developments on Dow Jones market (Jones & Khanna 2006). In the year 2015 there were a variety of events that had an impact on Dow Jones such as the Greek crisis, the drop of oil prices, as well as the shift that took place with regard to changes to the Federal Reserve interest rate policies,

Greek turmoil and the impact it has on Dow Jones

The time the Greek crisis hit, Dow Jones decreased to the lowest rate and was deemed to be the most disastrous day for the year 2015. The drastic drop was the result of Greece shutting down their banking system, the central bank controlling controls to prevent cash from leaving Greece as well as the protests that occurred because people were not happy with the changes in place (Consolandi 2009).

The selling process was mostly broad-based. The volume of trading was excessive at 7.3 billion shares constantly trading hands, as compared to the average annual data of six billion shares. The Dow industrials dipped by 350.33 points, or 17596.35. In contrast the S&P 500 fell to 43.85 points , to 2057.64. In addition the Nasdaq index fell to 122.04 in the range of 4958.47.

Figure 1. Dow Jones decline due to the Greek crisis

The source is CNN money

The price of oil has fallen

In August, the price of oil dropped below $40 a barrel, which was the first instance it has happened since 2009 amid a growing consensus that low-cost crude is likely to remain. Oil investors, who worked it out in the beginning that prices would rebound in the second half of the year, declare that price rebounds are likely to occur prior to the year. Forecasters for the government have lowered their estimates of the price of oil up to $65 per barrel over the course of the year 2016.

The shift in opinion is due in large part to the production of oil from the United States, who are continually increasing the amount of crude they pump. A surprise rally in prices in certain companies allowed companies to secure profit-making prices for the year 2016. Brent crude, the world benchmark, dropped by 2.5 percent to around $45.46 per barrel.

Figure 2: Effect of market fluctuations on the price of stocks

Source WSG

Federal Reserve interest rate policies

In the last quarter of 2015 at the end of 2015, in the year 2015 the Federal Reserve decided to increase interest rates. This has had a major impact on the market for stocks and, in particular, Dow Jones. It is the first time this has happened in the last nine years, and nobody anticipated the magnitude of this increase to occur. It had a positive effect on the stock market, as Down Jones increased by 185 points, Nasdaq increased by 1.1 percent while it was reported that the S&P 500 increased by 1.3 percentage. It was a unanimous vote to increase interest rates. Fed officially stated that when rates rise but the policy will remain accommodative. It is believed that the Federal Reserve policy has helped in boosting stock prices in the United States since the crisis began. The dollar has weakened in comparison to the Euro. Additionally, the yen's government bonds grew more expensive, bringing yields to a lower level. Stocks that pay dividends with a high value, that have risen continuously during the previous year amid low interest rates and a low interest rate, saw the S$P 500 gaining following the decision of the Feds. The cost of crude oil jumped by 4.9 each barrel with a sharp drop for two days, following an increase in oil supplies across the United States. The increase came quickly and wasn't anticipated in any way. On the other hand markets in other regions like Europe and Asia were not open for trading at the time they Federal Reserve released their new decision. This is among the rare instances which had a positive impact upon Dow Jones and associated trading processes throughout the year of 2015.

In 2015, there were a variety of circumstances which affected Dow Jones such as the Greek crisis, the decline in oil prices, and the shift that occurred in Federal Reserve interest rate policies. The report also provided an overview of diverse situations that impact Dow Jones. These include wars, natural catastrophes, and political incidents. Each of these events have both positive and negative impact. It can be difficult to figure out what will happen and whether traders are likely gain or lose the money. Although traders are able to predict certain events prior to them taking place, it's difficult to be able to do so in any situation, particularly in the case of natural catastrophes which are not known the exact time when they will occur. Additionally, it's difficult to know what kind of event will be likely to affect Dow Jones. In this study it is possible to find instances where wars, for instance, affected S & P positively and certain instances where it impacted the stock negatively.

Mutual Funds

Mutual funds can be a means for investors to store their money in one spot which can help improve purchasing power and lower expenses for execution. One of the disadvantages of mutual funds are the various fees that they entail. Every type of mutual fund require a fee and some even have sales fees in addition to management fees. If you decide for mutual funds to purchase, you must make sure you are aware of the charges you must pay as well as the requirements of the investment fund. It is crucial to know that you'll only be allowed to exchange mutual funds only once each day and this is when the markets are closed.

Exchange Traded Fund

The Exchange Traded Fund (ETF) is a finance innovation that is more recent than others investment instruments. The ETF puts mutual funds into an investment vehicle that trades similar to stocks and is based on the law of one price. The law of one price states that when two funds track the same exact item, then the gain and the returns from these investments is likely to be exactly the same. If, for instance, investments are priced too high, you are going to be able to sell these high-valued investments, and then utilize the proceeds to purchase more of the correctly priced investments. But, if you choose to invest in an ETF ensure that you be aware of what the investment being monitored is and also the quantity of ETF shares being bought and sold daily.

It is crucial to inquire on who sponsors ETF functions and ensure that the process is carried out correctly. Each of these investments are fantastic investments and each of them can be used in a comprehensive plan.

Real estate

The idea of investing in real estate has grown in popularity over the past 50 years and is now considered as one of the top investments. Although it is true that the market for real estate offers many possibilities for earning money, purchasing, or having real estate for your property, it is much more complicated than investing in bonds or stocks.

Basic rental properties

It is among the oldest investment methods. It involves buying a the property, and renting it out to tenants. Owners are accountable for mortgages and other costs associated with keeping the property. Landlords may charge additional rent to cover these expenses and also to generate an income for themselves. In addition, the property may be appraised by the value.

The main difference between rentals and other investment options is the amount of time and effort involved in maintaining the investment. If you purchase an investment, it's likely remain in your investment accounts and appreciate in value.

Real estate investment groups

Real property investment groups are similar to mutual funds used to rent properties, and are the ideal option for those who don't want the hassle of assuming the responsibility of landlords. A good example of this could be buying apartments and allowing investors to buy them through the business, thus becoming members of investment organizations. Investors who are single can have multiple or one complex. In exchange for this kind or management firm will be able to collect some of the rent per month. Although this is a secure way to join the market of real estate investment but many companies are vulnerable to the exact costs that affect the mutual fund industry.

Real Estate Trading

This is thought to be the wild side of real estate. Real estate investors buy properties for the intention of keeping them for a specified period of time, usually not longer than four months, with the intention of selling them to make profits. This method is referred to as flipping homes and is based on buying properties that are priced too low or located in markets that are hot. Property filters that are pure and unfiltered planning to invest money in real estate to improve it. the investment has to have intrinsic value, which means it will earn profit without alteration, or they will not even take it into the consideration. Flipping properties in this manner is generally considered to be a temporary investment. If property owners find themselves in situations where they are unable to sell their properties, the situation could be overwhelming since the investors do not have enough cashto are able to finance mortgages on their long-term properties. This could result in ongoing loss for real estate brokers who are unable to sell real estate in weak markets.

REITs

It is interesting to note the fact that property has existed around the world for a long time before our grandparents, so it's no unusual to find that Wall Street was successful in discovering a method to transform real estate into an asset that can be traded publicly. The term "real estate investment trust" (REIT) are formed when an entity (or the trust) uses the money of investors to manage and purchase income-producing properties. REITs can be purchased and sold through major types of exchanges just like other stocks. Businesses must pay 90 percent of their tax-deductible profits through dividends to keep its status as REITs.

Starting a small business as well as investing into them

Making investments in other start-ups

Investments in established businesses or new companies is a good investment that is more profitable than you think. The venture capital fund that is traded publicly generally invest in various companies, developing a portfolio of businesses that have the potential to succeed. With just one investment you will have access to an extensive portfolio of businesses that have cleared the tests for venture capital. There are a lot of opportunities to direct invest in companies that you've got an understanding or have experience with which you could exchange equity stakes in exchange for funds you offer.

Both types of investments carry the potential for risk that is out of proportion which is in line with the outsized benefits in the event that the venture proves to be profitable. It is therefore essential to the necessary research and then invest in these possibilities. Making investments through venture capital investment is the most sought-after option. It isn't necessary to quit your job or open an office. You'll just need to purchase shares.

Partner Up

Instead of investing only in businesses to acquire equity stakes, take it to the next stage and becoming an investor in a company which is already established. This could mean working in the company, and focusing on areas that founders do not have the time to do things like marketing and accounting. Or potentially be a bigger responsibility. It's not just likely to give you an experience in entrepreneurship, but it will also allow you to choose the kinds of tasks you'd like to complete.

Intrapreneurship

Another option is to become an intrapreneur in larger firms. A lot of companies have established mechanisms that encourage employees to take on new organizational lines, in exchange for bonuses and equity. If you come across an organization with an energizing innovation culture, you will to be able to create your own business within it. You will also enjoy the advantage of having startup capital at the beginning, and your personal risk will be able to be reduced as well.

You may even be able to start an interpretership program at work, by requesting a certain amount of time to complete projects that come with bonuses structures. To make your case stronger you could always appeal your appeal to companies like 3M and Intel two firms that had significant growth over an era when the concept of interpretership was central to the corporate culture.

Buy an franchise

Boxes for businesses are one method to avoid the headaches of starting from scratch. Franchise owners follow a set of rules that have proved to be successful. The benefits of franchises are having a brand that is well-known with resources that they can go into, as well as the economies of scale that franchises create.

The primary drawback is the price of buying the franchise and the fees, which are high often. People who want to have the full business experience are likely to encounter issues with the various restrictions that franchise offices add to their. But, they usually offer a strong support system and are renowned for having the highest success rates.

Chapter 2: Make a Sense of Yourself

Get the confidence you need to realize that you have to make a commitment to yourself to make cash. Not only do you possess the knowledge and experience to run your own business however, you'll also be confident that you possess a uniqueness that makes you stand out from others. We all have something we're adept at. Sometimes, it's easy to spot, while sometimes, it requires greater distance from an outsider's viewpoint or an extended contemplation to determine the thing that makes us apart from others. The desire to get off your financial burdens and invest in your future will help you recognize your uniqueness. There are plenty of people who are living their lives with no enthusiasm, motivation or desire to make a difference. better. You realize that you don't just wish to be better however, you are entitled to be better than you are.

Examine your talents as a creative and determine if there's something you can make money doing by yourself. Are you adept in drawing? Have you got a green thumb? Maybe music is your thing. Whatever you are passionate about, it are able to call your own and that you love there's a way you can use it to your advantage. If you're unable to maintain your interest in the art on your own, maybe you can teach the craft to someone else. If we put our money into ourselves, not only do we discover ways to earn money doing something we love doing and enjoy, but we also develop yourself by putting the emphasis on a personal passion. Instead of working for an individual all day it is a job on your own behalf, so while you're earning money, you're growing into a healthier, better and more content person.

Treat yourself as an investment. Make healthier choices. Consider the quality of your life in terms of investment. It is possible to eat unhealthy food right now, but it's likely to become more difficult for your body as you age. In the present there's a chance that you don't have any health issues, but there may be something that is cutting years off your planned life. Ingestion of too many fatty meals can cause heart disease. Smoking cigarettes can be costly and has a track record of reducing your life expectancy each time you smoke smoking a cigarette. They are enjoyable but we all have times where we'd like to indulge in the greatest. The same habits can come back and impact your life negatively as you grow older.

It's much easier to focus on the present moment and the way we live our lives because of the current events happening around us. We are able to put the future off of our minds. We cannot live in that way any longer, which is why we need to look at your bodies as personal investment.

Have a positive attitude about this. You must be confident enough to believe that you're the most influential person in your life. It isn't always the truth and you shouldn't get obsessed with trying to please everyone else. There are people who don't want to or won't be interested in your work However, that doesn't suggest that you don't possess merit. If you're experiencing problems, take a look at the issue from a different angle. You can always find a method you can fix something positively instead of turning it into an unhelpful negative. Sometimes, you may think that you're not valuable or have committed a mistake, but you could put a positive spin to it, which can make you feel better in the end.

Don't wait for things to occur. It's up to you to manage your financial situation. Many people awake in the morning wondering about the reasons they're unhappy and, rather than doing anything to change it, they just keep doing the work they don't like and return home exhausted and unable to do anything other than to get ready for the next day. Some people recognize they're unhappy, and consider what they can do to improve their lives regardless of how small. If you start investing your time and your time into making you healthier and happier you'll begin to see the amount of things you've missed out on.

Don't place too much pressure on yourself. It's not a good idea to talk about yourself in a manner that is insulting or demeaning. If we place excessive stress on ourselves we can end getting even more stressed to meet our own standards when we don't achieve our lofty expectations. To ensure that we don't destroy confidence in ourselves it is important to ensure that we're setting reasonable goals and accepting that we'll have not meet our goals or make deadlines. We're more knowledgeable than everyone else that we're not perfect however, we can also be more mean to ourselves than to the majority of other people. To ensure that we don't fall into a state of over-confidence it is essential to adhere to goals that are feasible. That's why it's crucial to begin with modest savings and begin to put more money in the savings account.

Concentration and Studying

Knowledge is power, particularly when you are dealing with your personal financial situation. The more you are aware of how to manage and save money the easier it will be to make educated decisions. Keep in mind that not everyone can become a financial expert within a short time. Don't jump in to something that you don't know, since it is where mistakes could be made and mistakes can happen. Be sure you're aware of the entire subject before you dive in. If you're in way too much and don't know the whole story, you'll end up losing money, therefore it's essential to be well-informed and know how to deal with any scenario that might fail.

Be aware that the more you begin to master and grow, the more you realize that there is so much more to discover. It is possible to become extremely proficient in real estate within an area for instance but the more you are immersed into that particular region and the more you realize that there is plenty to learn about other locations also. It can be difficult to be more educated and knowledgeable about specific areas of investment since it will feel as if there is a lot to be learned. The best thing to do instead is beginning small and working on the fundamentals. Do not be afraid to search for the precise meaning of specific words, even if they think you've heard them in your entire life. It is important to know things in their natural context to avoid getting too lost. The realm of finance particularly with regards to investments is full of experts than you and more naive too, so you could get stuck in a situation which could be prevented.

Make sure you choose your sources carefully. There's a wealth of information which can be misleading and some can be persuasive either way. When you're reading an article that has "shocking" facts, make sure you read all sources. More frequently than not these headlines are just hyperbole to make you go to the website and read more. Some sources are more favorable of an result, so they'll portray the opposing perspective as frightening or negative, and you will be a part of their view. It's a tangled world online, and it can be difficult to remember all data that is fair and truthful. With regards to investing money don't be aware of the ways certain media sources may twist things, you could end with a loss on your investment.

Only focus on your goals and not others. Each of us has our own unique routes and journeys which we're likely to travel along and follow throughout our lives. What is even more different is the final destination we'll be waiting for at the close of the road. We all are aware of the goals we wish to achieve in life at an early stage, and others are left to wonder what their goals to be exactly. Determining these aspects of our lives can be difficult enough, and some are drawn to the thoughts and objectives of other people in an effort to establish a connection to any level. They are desperate to answer the many questions they need to answer. Do not get caught up in the goals of others. Be sure you're clear on what you want and following the right steps to achieve it and not just to achieve an idea that someone else has of what it takes to be successful or happy.

Do not let too much fantasies get in the way of. Don't, in particular, let yourself be entangled in any fantasies that are fantastical. It is important to remain realistic. It's easy to get caught up in the notion of what could be. Now, you could dream of owning 3 cars, 2 homes as well as a boat and an entire family that is picture perfect. The possibilities are endless in our heads and if we imagine all the positive that is possible then we'll be lost in a thought that's a fantasies. We must ensure we're not becoming lost in the haze of what could perhaps, maybe, be. Keep to the facts and make small steps so that you can be real. The ultimate objective is a general notion that is similar, but the goals you set and achieve may change a little as you travel. For instance when you'd like to be millionaire, that's something you aren't able to set a specific date for. However, you can imagine that you're planning to have $25,000 of your savings at the date of X during the year. This could change by one or two months however, that's fine as you're still on the right the right track in general. It's a realistic goal, but your constant fantasies about what's likely to happen when you're millionaire may keep you from reaching the smaller objectives that are necessary to reach your goals.

If you are in need of an expert in business don't be afraid seek out an expert. There are those who are educated in business with the ability that they are able to provide an objective opinion on what you should do to achieve success. There are bankers, lawyers, accountants, and business executives who will assist you whenever you require it. They will provide insight and suggestions to ensure that you're spending funds in the most intelligent manner you can. Some people prefer doing things on their own, and not completely trusting someone else with their money. Keep in mind that this is their responsibility and even although there are bad individuals out there You can trust the experts who are trained to do what is best for you. Always be able to rely on someone to assist you in the beginning of your investment and business ventures for example, an experienced business manager or broker.

Instilling belief and passion

Sometimes, trusting in ourselves is the most difficult part of getting over our own mistakes. Even if you require assistance get started however, it doesn't suggest that you're incapable of becoming your own boss later on. If we live our lives and do not achieve much we may make us feel like we're not worthy of much, haven't achieved the ability to succeed, or have no right to be doing better. If you've not had any success in your own life but that doesn't mean that there isn't there If you are determined and set goals that are achievable. It begins with believing that you're capable of anything, and knowing that your past doesn't need to dictate what you will do in the future.

We're told that we need to rely on large corporations to get money. We're deceived by our own assumptions. We watch billionaires and successful entrepreneurs and think that we're not having as good of an idea and that it's unlikely we'll successful enough to achieve that level of success. What's the point of it if we cannot become as successful or famous as Warren Buffet or Jeff Bezos? We must remember however is that everybody started out with a small amount of money. Nobody can claim that they were born successful because the amount of money you earn does not determine success. It's the way you use your resources and how prepared you are to take on challenges, which is what really counts in determining success.

We must be humble when it comes to our goals. We all get lucky in certain circumstances and may receive things we never imagined when we started the process. While you're investing keep in mind the time when you had only two dimes to mix together. There was a time that you were less than the amount you have today and, if you're not skilled, you will be able to get back to the point you were at. Keep your eyes on the prize of your own self-worth and never forget your journey that led you to where you reached your goal. If you're able to remain grounded and recall the reason that led you to this point way in the first place It will be more easy to remain committed to your goals and will result in your success later on. A lot of people fail in the event that they fail to remember what the goal of their endeavor was to begin with.

Who we surround ourselves is equally important. There are many people who will not be able to assist your financial needs, but anyone who claims to are in love with or respect for you will be able to inspire and help you. People who have been there to help you in the beginning are going become the best. Anyone who discourages you, diminishes you, and discredits you won't be an individual who can help you along your investment journey. If you don't have anyone who will support you, it may be difficult to maintain and achieve your success. Be sure to surround your self with those who are most important to you and that you don't let anyone stand behind you in achieving your goals.

Passion is what will assist you in achieving your goals. It is essential to be passionate about the topic you're investing your money into. If you are doing this it will make sure that you are taking care of the end result. It is important to be supportive of your actions and believe in the purpose of the venture you're investing in. If you do not care about your investment, it's likely to be difficult to keep relationships going and maintain the earnings momentum that you're experiencing when you start a business using different investment options. If you don't have the motivation to manage their investments aren't good managers and may eventually be disconnected from their business.

A lot of enthusiasm for investing will assist in making sure we've got the right mindset to persevere even those times where we haven't achieved our goals. If you're prone to giving up because the thing you're taking part in isn't appealing to you, then you'll constantly fail. We must instead be sure we're enthusiastic about the topic of investing so that it's easier to stay current with latest developments and news in the area. This is the reason investing in yourself is extremely beneficial. If you're doing something that you are passionate about you'll find it more easy to become emotionally and financially invested in something.

Understanding the Game

You make an investment when you anticipate to earn something back typically, a greater amount than the initial investment. Making money simply offering money may seem like a fantastic idea but there's much beyond the idea of making money. It is important to ensure that you're considering results, work and a host of other elements before committing to invest. The challenge is to find the perfect equilibrium between security and risk and trust, and how much effort. It's not as easy as paying money and hoping to be rewarded at the end. It's what you're going to receive back which is worth it at the end of the day.

It's a challenging game that requires you to be more strategically. It is not possible to enter a field without knowing the basics of the topic or else you're likely to find it difficult to make money. It's not something that is easy to talk about However, it's also certain that there are those who could be able to profit from your vulnerability. They are able to speak quick and confidently about something in order to convince people to accept their ideas. It's not always possible to expect this will work at the end of the day, however. Some individuals may make a profit of you and let you go without a penny even though they had originally stated that they would provide all they could.

Each type of investment comes with their own set of rules and guidelines. There are laws which try to shield your investment from any mishaps. Some people continue to do illegal things and may even encourage others to do the same. Be aware that if something is illegal, it's never worth the effort at the end. You won't be able to expect success if you are attempting to cheat others to get money, or taking something that isn't yours. This goes far beyond legal, and can lead to moral issues like underpaid employees or those who have to perform more than they can do for their particular job. You must ensure that you're adhering to strict moral and legal guidelines so that you do not need to be concerned about being in trouble or harming another person. Risk is a part of investing however if the risk is being caught in a crime or going to jail, or taking money that's not yours, it's not worthy of the risks.

In the first place, you must ensure that you're only engaging in legal investments. When you work with other investors ensure that you have your own legal team prior to engaging with them. You shouldn't use only lawyers working under their advisor since even lawyers are at a loss to follow a certain direction. Before investing in large amounts it is crucial to have someone who is legally with you. In this way, they'll be able to offer you objective advice and crucial opinions that ensure your financial security and protection.

There is a degree of perseverance that you need to possess when investing. While it's tempting to believe that you can just put all your money into all at once to earn the most lucrative return, that is not the way things happen. It is important to be patient and the willpower to go slow initially to ensure that you don't make any errors. It could take many years to save a certain sum of cash, however it could all go to waste in the event that you dispose of it in the wrong spot. Don't let all your hard work be wasted due to a poor investment choice.

There's a fine line between taking huge risks and being safely too. This is the most difficult aspect of the game you'll need to become used to. Even the most wealthy and successful investors may not find this balance easily discernible in their investment portfolios. Certain things are more difficult than others and you must be sure you're being as objective as you can and still have the passion and the courage to take the appropriate risk. Sometimes, your risk pays huge, while at some times, you could be forced to take losses. It's all part the game, but.

The Passive Income Method and the Way to Make It

Many people believe that passive income is just lying around on the couch, and just laying around in a circle while cash is coming into. This is far from the reality. Although passive income implies that you aren't actively involved however it does not mean that you're that you're not doing anything at all. What exactly is"passive income?

The word"passive" usually signifies 'not active'. passive income is the result of earning money while not being actively engaged.

The truth is that for you to earn passive income, you'll need to invest in work, money or even time. There are times when you invest in all the above.

Passive income refers to the money you receive after the work is completed. It could include royalties earned from a music or movie or book. Also, it could include the income from investments, such as real estate, and other businesses. It's the moment that you reach where your assets are earning you income even when you're not present. However, it is not something that can be achieved in a single day. If you hear stories about earning passively, you might be tempted to believe that it's easy as beginning a blog, creating the eBook and uploading your track to YouTube and then earning. This isn't the case for any of the reasons. This is definitely not a strategy for earning money in the short term.

Passive income can bring financial freedom and freedom. This means that you don't be required to work in a cubicle all day.

Passive income is for everyone who would like to earn an extra source of income. It is not important if you're a successful businessman with brilliant ideas for entrepreneurship or a budding artist. It is not a matter of magic in passive earnings. The seeds you plant will sprout and develop over time. Certain passive income options will require lots of work before you are able to earn. Some, for instance, involve an Robo advisor since it requires less effort.

Ideas for passive income

There's a vast collection of possibilities that you can look into when thinking about passive income. When you think about every idea you can think about the amount of work each idea requires and the potential returns.

It is also important to remember that you might not make a lot of money if you only implement one idea. You are able to look over the possible possibilities and choose those you believe is the most beneficial for you.

Below are some ideas you could explore:

Investing In Crowdfunded Real Estates

When we hear the word "real estate the first thing that comes to our minds first is rental properties and how to purchase one. Making investments in real estate directly involves a significant amount. The execution of a single project requires a large amount of capital. It can also consume the majority of your time even if you use an outside contractor to handle all aspects. But the reality is that it is possible to get into real estate for $500 in cash.

Crowdfunded real estate makes real estate no longer just only for the wealthy. It's possible for everyone from the average people. You loan your money to a developer or landlord or real estate company that purchases the property. They then pay a specific interest on your cash.

The benefit is that you can put it into investment together with many others.

RealtyShares is an internet-based platform you can utilize. It's a site that lets real estate businesses that need money to finance their projects to connect with potential investors to purchase shares in the particular project.

Reit is a business that lets you make investments in the real estate investments through the purchase of shares. Then, you will receive an amount of the earnings from the investment. There is no requirement to own a home to make money with REITs.

Fundraiser offers you the possibility to invest on commercial properties using eREIT that operates as an online service. Investors of all levels can invest just $500. Additionally, the fees are lower when compared to regular Reit.

Worthy Bonds Investment

The investment in Worthy bonds will help you reduce your expenses and increase your earnings. If you purchase bonds for corporations and earn an annual interest of 5. The money earned from Worthy bonds are used to finance small-scale businesses in America which require capital to expand. This means that you invest while helping someone else to grow their business. You are also in control of the time you wish to invest and the amount you're willing to contribute. This is because you are able to return your bonds anytime.

It is possible to do this manually or in daily round-ups.

To earn money with Worthy bond, purchase the bonds through Worthy (seller). Worthy will then loan the money to borrowers, who return the loan with interest. After that, the investment is returned to you with the interest rate of 5.

Savings with a High-Interest Rate Account

It is sometimes viewed as boring investing. This kind of investment might not bring you wealth in a hurry However, it's safe and more secure. The accounts pay modest interest. Sometimes , it's as the low of 0.05 percent on your deposit.

To earn through this method, deposit your savings into a savings account. There are many banks on the internet that have these accounts. The most effective market accounts have higher rates of interest.

Affording CDs (Certificate of Deposit) is another alternative. They're simple and easy to use. CDs are similar to savings accounts, but with a twist. You deposit the money and establish a period of time. You aren't able to take your savings out until they are mature. This is dependent on the time frame you choose to decided to set. The period could be months or even years. The CD investment has fewer risk. It is because the CDs have a fixed rate of interest rate that isn't dependent on fluctuations in market interest.

Create an online course

Do you have specialization in a specific subject? The knowledge you have can earn you a little extra cash. All you have to do is put your knowledge into an online course , and then market it.

You can sell or host the course on websites such as Teachable as well as Udemy. They already have a following, and all you have to do is make amazing, well-written content that is easily shared and provides value to the people who view it.

You could also provide the course as a download link on your blog or on your website, and advertise it on social media platforms.

If, for instance, you are an expert on public speaking for instance, you could develop an online course called "Public speaking

Demystified" which you can then provide it on the internet. The benefit of having online courses is that once you've created the content that you will need for your course you'll be able to sell it online, and there is no limit to how much you'll make from it.

Write An eBook

Writing eBooks are a great opportunity to make passive money. It could require more effort than other income streams that are passive however it's an option worth exploring.

To make money from writing eBooks, you have to:

Choose a topic and subject. Writing about topics that interest you will make your writing more natural and helps keep you interested. But, ensure that the subject that you choose to write on is something that you could commercialize. You could research affiliate programs that pay high commissions and create an eBook about specific products that you believe will help the customer.

Find the affiliate programs. Affiliate programs help promote the products of a business. Sign up to advertise and promote a product of a company and you are then given an exclusive code. Your code is placed in your eBook whenever you get a client to purchase an item through your link, you receive a fee for this.

Make your own eBook

You can write your ebook and then find ways to market it. It can be done through Facebook groups or on online platforms like the Amazon Kindle Store.

You could also opt to combine a few free articles into a book. Then, you are the publisher.

Following that, you will include affiliate links for the items you would like to advertise. The advertisements will appear as the reader is reading. Customers who are interested will click the links and buy the items. This is when you can earn commissions.

Distribute the book

The eBook can be distributed in a variety of ways:

Emailing this to the list on your emails.

Downloading a link to your website

Promoting it on social media platforms, such as Facebook, Twitter, etc

- Using free eBook websites

Bloggers can offer the items for free to anyone who go to their blogs

Investing In Dividends

Dividends are the portion of profits earned by a business over time. Dividends are determined by the Board of Directors. The companies pay dividends in the form of shares, property or cash.

The amount you receive as dividends will depend on the profits that you can share as well as the amount of stock you own in the business.

Dividends can be a reliable passive income strategy to take into consideration. It is possible to reinvest dividends into the company to purchase more stocks to earn higher return in the near future.

Peer-to-peer Lending

Another option is to those looking for an income stream that is passive. Similar to banks, you can lend money to be repaid with interest. It connects prospective borrowers with lenders. This is beneficial for the borrowers who may not be able to get loan from banks due to certain factors such as having no credit history.

They can also make money from high interest rates, which can be greater than 10 percent.

An excellent illustration can be found in Lending Club, which acts as an intermediary between lenders as well as borrowers.

The benefit of working with lenders clubs as lenders is that you get an enviable share of interest paid by the club. It is the responsibility of the business to make sure that the borrower is able to repay the loan.

The upgrade is identical to Lending Club, but it is more stringent. In this upgrade, the borrower is graded so that they know the amount they are able to take out. The amount they are able to be able to borrow will depend the credit scores as well as the ratio of their debt to income. The score also determines the interest rate at which the borrower will be charged. It also determines if one can be considered a loan applicant or not.

The Benefits of Investing in Index Funds

Index Funding is a different income stream that is passive. It is important to be aware that there are both good and bad indexes. To avoid falling in the trap of the negative index, you must consider trading with a reputable management firm. If you're a novice investor, you must look for an index that is low-cost and passive.

Rent Out Space

For that extra money without much effort, renting the extra room or even your home is a smart idea. It could be as easy as finding a roommate take over the extra space or renting it to traveller strangers. Between the two the latter is more than passive. But sharing economies can offer a fantastic opportunity to earn extra income. It is, however, possible that you require precautions to ensure your safety and security as there are times when you will be hosting guests from outside.

It is possible to rent the spare bedroom you don't use or basement garage garden, driveway, etc. They can be used for different reasons, like creating a studio and parking, for social gatherings or camping.

It's a passive income venture that requires no effort, as the space is already accessible and ready to be set up. It can be used to reduce your mortgage payments and also secure your home. For those who are determined in acquiring connections, it has become their full-time job , earning good income.

Airbnb allows people to travel around across the globe and find accommodation for less than hotels. Airbnb classifies their rental properties as private homes, shared home, or the whole home. The company charges 3.3% per bookingand for up to 24 hours after guests have been checked in, you will receive the payment.

When you offer an Airbnb space to rent it is important that you get a good review from your guests. Reviews can be a big deal for you. They are one of the most important factors in increasing the number of clients.

How to become a Social Media Influencer

If you're a media influencer, you could earn a decent income. It might not be entirely passive venture initially but as your reach grows, it could become a profitable business. Being an influential social media user with a large following means companies are aware of you and may approach you to become an ambassador for their brands. They may also reach out to you to promote their product. If you have your own blog and are an influencer on social media You can mix affiliate and advertising programs to make more.

Be a Rideshare Driver

Being a rideshare driver might appear to be a passive activity. However, it is extremely flexible, which makes it a passive job. You can create your own plan and you earn cash taking people around. You could take on passengers traveling towards the same destination and earn extra cash.

Business buying

The process of starting a business and bringing the business to enormous heights isn't a stroll through the crowd. It requires investment, commitment as well as a lot of effort and work. Avoid the hassle by purchasing an established company. Someone might not have the funds to run their business, and might offer for auction. If you have the money to purchase it and not have to go through the initial step of beginning the business and attempting to gain exposure.

Outsource the Business

If your company does not include products or services that you are the only one who can provide and sell, you could transform it into an income-generating venture that is passive as you focus on other aspects. This can be done by hiring reliable employees who will be able to run the business even in the absence of you.

You could also think about hiring people who are ethical and trustworthy that will work for you under a contract.

The main point is that regardless of whether you have millions to invest, or you don't, passive revenue will help you. It can take some time to build and expand however, eventually you'll be able to benefit from the income with minimal effort. Therefore, whether you choose to become an influencer on social media purchase a business or rent out your space, or even join the real estate industry and plant the seeds.

Chapter 3: Are you interested in pursuing a career?

Interest is classified into two types one: the kind you pay and the kind you earn. It can be beneficial as when you accumulate an interest rate within your bank account. It can also be detrimental as when you are owed money due to your credit cards. Here are a few ways in which interest can be a part of your daily life.

If you borrow: Pay the amount you borrowed and also the interest

When you savemoney: The bank will reward you with interest to keep your savings in the bank. This permits them to loan to other bank members.

When you lend money: You establish the interest rate and profit from the money you loan.

Wait, wait, wait. The bank will provide us with money to put our money into their bank What?! There are other alternatives that could earn you additional cash? !

These incredible, money-making accounts are referred to as high interest savings accounts. Savings accounts that earn high interest are beneficial due to the greater amount of interest you earn for every dollar you put in.

It's not a simple interest

What is the definition of simple interest?

Simple interest is the interest you earn over time, based solely on the amount that you put in.

What?

Let's dissect it with an equation.

To calculate the simple interest simply, you need to multiply the amount with the interest rate , and then the amount of time. If I deposit $1 into the bank and earn 10 percent interest. Since that interest rates can be described as decimal points we'll have the conversion from 10% into decimal. Take the decimal, and shift it to the left two times! After we add these two numbers and we'll have a figure that's 10% of our initial deposit. Add it all up and pretend that interest is paid out each month, and we'll have the amount!

1 (our $1) 1 x .10 (10 percent interest) * 12 (we are interested in determining how much we earn over the course of a one year) = 1.2

In the course of a year we'll earn $1.20 just by keeping the cash at the banks! The result will be $2.20!

It is essential to be aware of interest since there's both good and negative interest. When you decide to get a loan you must be aware of the interest rates. This could significantly impact the ability of you to repay it. If the rate of interest is excessive, you could be unable to pay back the amount you initially took out.

But, it's not the only type of interest that exists. There's compound interest, too. This is the kind of interest that is earned in addition to interest. It's great when you have an account for savings that is producing interest on top of interest since your savings will surely increase quicker. The compound interest may be more difficult for us when it's the amount we owe. If you are charged an interest rate that is compounded on your loan it's very difficult to even get any progress in repaying the initial amount.

The most effective compound interest investments:

Certificates of deposit

High-interest savings accounts

Rental properties

Bonds (see chapter three)

Stocks (see chapter three)

Treasury securities: If the government requires money to pay its debts, or has plans for something entirely new, you may purchase Treasury bills. And when you wait until it becomes mature, you'll benefit from it.

And then there are the other potential pitfalls we'd rather not have to have. The interest we pay on our credit cards. If you're applying for a credit card and you're approved and you are able to begin buying things like we discussed earlier in order to improve your credit score. Be careful not to go over your budget or make a major purchase in the knowledge that you do not have enough money to repay it. The best method to stay prudent with your credit card while building credit is to make a small amount of purchases and pay the balance off. The interest that accumulates from an account with a credit card could be as high as 20% or more So be cautious of what you spend!

As it is wise to keep the balance of your credit card at a minimum or even to zero, it's important to be aware of any loans we take out. If they're sourced from a reliable company and when the interest and financing rates are not excessively expensive, we can be more assured about the direction our money will go.

Let's discuss equity

Equity is the amount you pay for the assets you own after deducting the amount you owe to it.

There are two kinds of equity:

Book Value: There's an equation for calculating market equity. It is assets less liabilities. Assets are what you have and liabilities are what you have to pay.

Market Value: The term "equity" can be defined in terms of market value. It includes the amount you've invested in the stock market, and the market value is always changing due to investors, shareholders, etc.

You may have heard of, the mortgage. It's a type of loan that you obtain when you wish to buy a house. Mortgages pay interest that is simple but since you're paying interest upfront the time to pay off the principle which is the amount that you initially borrowed. This is the same for the cost of a car. The majority of car dealerships determine the interest rate based on the credit score you have. In the event that you've got a expensive interest, you is more difficult to pay the principal.

Equity prices can fluctuate between up and down, but there are certain aspects that fluctuate between the two. What happens when value increases?

Things like your home can increase in value in time. It is possible to purchase a house that requires work or repairs, and if you've got the time and expertise then you can make it by making a few improvements and the value of your house will rise. Another reason that houses increase significantly in value is that there aren't enough homes being constructed to meet the rising demand.

What happens when value decreases?

Things like cars decrease in value, or even depreciate. Based on current rates that a car could depreciate by over 20% in just one year. The car will continue decline at approximately 10% per year over the following four years. At the end of the five-year period of owning you're in the position that your car will be worth around 40% of the amount that you initially paid the car (Car Depreciation: What Causes New Cars Depreciate So quickly? n.d.-b).

This is due to the fact that the parts of the car don't endure the wear and wear and tear. The demand for cars isn't as great as that of housing. There are new cars coming out every year, which can affect what you can expect to get for your vehicle. The resale value is too low. When your car is removed from the lot, it's considered to be used.

The most efficient way to save money isn't to buy a new. Although it may appear to be the most ideal option but you will save more over the long haul when you choose to buy an old car. If you can save to the full amount of the car or purchase an older model, and then get the bank loan with lower rate of interest, you'll be far better off. Make sure to do thorough research to ensure that your vehicle is in good shape. Get a mechanic in to look over the car and make sure that nothing is likely to be a problem before too long. In the final, it's better to hire an expert once to ensure you're in a secure vehicle.

Real Estate

A home purchase is one of the biggest decisions you'll make throughout your life. It's a achievement that many try to reach. The ability to pay off your mortgage earlier than later is what people aim for. This requires lots of research, not just on the market and pricing however, but also on the neighbors and the community.

Additional tips to find your perfect home:

Take into consideration the location and whether there are any amenities in the vicinity such as supermarkets or other malls for shopping.

Be sure that you're not in a community that is populated by tenants.

Take a look at the neighborhood and see determine if it's safe in crime.

Take into consideration the location and if you would like to be close to family members, or not.

Your budget must be put into the picture because certain areas have higher prices for living than others.

The weather may be significant to you, therefore when you aren't a fan of extreme cold or hot weather take note of this.

In the event that you own pets, you should consider purchasing a house that has a beautiful backyard.

A school close to your home could be something you'll want to be thinking about.

If you don't have any vehicle, you can research transportation routes and see whether they're convenient within your local area.

There are many words in the field of real estate you must be familiar with to assist you in understanding the procedure.

Appraisal: This will determine the value of your house in the moment of purchase , and how your mortgage will appear like following.

Buyer's agent: This person assists the buyer in sales.

Market for buyers: It is the place where supply is greater than demand, and the buyers have an advantage over sellers.

Closing Sale property is conclusive.

Guarantee for your home in the event of unexpected expenses for plumbing or other related expenses it will be covered by renters.

Checking: It is a must to carry out prior to buying an investment property in order to ensure that all is in good standards.

Pre-approval letter The lender will send an email to the buyer to inform them that they're able to get money.

Market analysis of real estate This is a study carried out to find out the market's potential to be profitable.

Realtor: They assist you buy or sell an asset, and they are highly experienced in the area of real estate.

Refinancing: You could receive lower interest rates by swapping an old mortgage for an entirely new one.

Market for sellers: It is when there is a lower demand or shortage of properties, therefore sellers benefit more than buyers.

Costs for closing: These include expenses like taxes and other processing fees and expenses you must pay at the time of closing on a home.

Market analysis by Comparative: The purpose of this is done to examine the value of other homes around to determine the value on the market

Foreclosure: The lender takes your house if you fail to pay your mortgage

It is crucial to understand that you will have demand and supply depending on specific demographics, the economic situation, or the housing market collapses. It is important to conduct thorough research before you are looking to buy an apartment, and keep an eye on the price trends and in the various market conditions. Remember, once you are in the process enjoy yourself!

Chapter 4: Be aware of your Money Habits

Every investment requires capital. This means that you cannot put money into something without investing time and effort. The money you're planning to invest comes because of your effort. It's not something that can be thrown out of the blue. It's something you've earned on your own. A lot of people are unable to invest due to absence of the funds they require to begin something. To get rid of this issue is to understand your financial habits. Understanding the different types of investments in the first chapter is just the beginning of building your routine. After you've chosen the kind of path you're planning to take for your investment, you now need to set an objective in your head. This will assist you in creating your financial habits. In reality, there are some tips you can apply to conserve capital for your investment.

Limit the amount you spend on credit

Credit cards have helped make the lives of many simpler. Indeed, the majority of people today prefer using credit cards to pay for their bills rather than cash. The debt isn't a problem to be concerned about. Some banks will even grant enormous privileges to their customers particularly if they're good customers. But, sometimes, credit cards become a trap for the individual. If you don't keep track of your spending habits, you may encounter financial problems in the near future. According to an investigation, 38.1% of households in the US are in debt because of the misuse of credit cards. If you can reduce your debts on credit cards and avoiding debt, you'll be able save not just yourself from future problems, but also your investments.

Make use of a money tracker

There are numerous applications users can install to monitor your expenses and income. Remember that the goal is to establish a routine to "saving." When you're conscious of your expenses, you can make sure you save some of your earnings for an investment. Each day, record your expenses and take notes. This way, you'll be able budget your expenses for the entire month or week based on the routine you choose. You can also save the statements from your credit card or receipts. Remember that this tip is crucial since the majority of our spending comes through small purchases that we often forget about. If you can track your expenses the exact amount of your expenses, you will be able identify which items account for the largest portion of your expenditure.

Learn to make a reserve

The most efficient way to make cash for investing is to put aside a small portion of your income starting from the day you receive it. For instance, if you earn an income that is $1,000 every month you could put aside $100 to fund savings. You can also open a different bank account that is different to your paycheque account to ensure you won't be capable of spending your savings, even though you already have it in your account. If you're not confident with the idea of setting aside money prior to your first payday, you can choose to do it in a different way. You could set aside funds after you've made all of your expenditures and purchases. But, remember that there's a amount of psychology involved in saving. The more you think that you have money to invest, the higher the likelihood you'll be unable to save.

It is recommended to save money before you spend. It is not a must to save a certain amount, as long as you're saving to fund your investment. The most important thing is that you're saving to yourself.

Check your budget and expenses

Review your budget and expenses. Ask yourself questions such as "what do I have in my budget to this month? ", "what is my top priority expense? ", "what are my requirements and wants?". If you take the time to examine your own habits to be able to establish an awareness of yourself. A few people also engage in the habit of saving the budget into categories for the costs. If they earn 1,000 dollars per month, they'll allocate their budget for each category. For instance,

House Rent $300

Food $300

Utilities - - $200

Miscellaneous - $100

Savings $200

Total $1000

By establishing budgets for each category it is more easy to get the most money you can spend for your needs. Also, it will aid you in saving money, while still utilizing your budget to save. It is also essential to be able to distinguish desires from requirements. Many people struggle with understanding the need and the wants. When you purchase a product, always ask yourself questions such as "Do I really need this right now?" and "Is this a desire or a requirement?" If you believe that the product isn't really necessary and you're not sure, don't purchase it. Instead, save it for yourself.

Another thing to examine is your regular utility bills. A lot of people do not realize that their internet or electricity bills may cost just a couple of dollars. This is due to the fact that people tend to overlook the small fees and charges that are included in utility bills. Have you ever looked over the details of your internet bill? If so, then you're doing well. If not, perhaps you should begin studying it. Every month you get your bill, make an effort to find out what the charges are. For instance, if you pay for a cable service every month, determine if there are channels that you're paying for, even though you do not make use of it in any way. You can also contact the company that handles the utility bills if you discover any hidden charges are not necessary to pay for. This will allow you to lower the amount you pay and also make your savings more substantial.

Conserve your utilities

Imagine that you step out of your bedroom and you forget to switch off the lights. There are instances when you fall asleep watching the TV and woke awake an hour after to discover that you didn't switch off the light. The fact that you're able to pay for your utility bills does not mean you can not take care to save it. A habit of conserving your energy usage doesn't just help you save a handful of dollars but it also helps to conserve the earth. In addition to the standard shutting off electrical appliances, it is possible that you can consider other options like using natural lighting to warm your home.

Learn to pack meals

As we live living in an "instant" world, where everything is accessible in a flash, many people prefer to buy food from outside rather instead of cooking for themselves. However, this can cost an enormous amount of money. Food is an essential item and is not a matter of choice when you are budgeting. Even if some snacks cost only a tiny amount but they are still one of your costs. The best method to avoid having to overspend on food is to bring snacks or meals. There are times when we simply want to take in the moment and indulge in some expensive food. This isn't bad in any way. But, if you're doing this several every month, you might want to cut it down so that you still save for future investment.

Another thing you can try is to ensure that you're well-fed when you visit a supermarket. According to a study those that are starving when they visit the grocery store tend to purchase more than people with a full stomach. The more you look at food items in the grocery store and the more you'll likely purchase it as you're hungry and your brain is trying to convince you into buying it at the moment.

Do not spend it when you are at the top in your feelings.

Did you notice that the malls offer sales for payday? This is due to the fact that customers could purchase it in that particular time. Remember that it is a scam. A mall strategy can encourage customers to buy items aren't needed or purchase if it's on sale. This type of scenario is known as Emotional Spending. Emotional spending is the result of the successful sales strategies employed by businesses. There are times that you are prone to purchase or shop for items when you are feeling lonely or alone. This is because shopping is a source of joy, even if you don't really require these products in the first place. When you're in the midst emotion, you are likely to overlook the budget you've established for yourself. People see buying things as a way to unwind. However, there are many different ways that you can unwind and not spend a dime. You can visit an area park, wander through your neighborhood, or sit at home and watch a film. Remember it is not a good thing to perform even if the goal is simply to take in the sights. This isin reality riskier and could be risking your savings. Remember that firms know how to attract you , and the best method to save money is to steer clear of these sales, especially in cases where you do not need those products in the first place.

Unsubscribe from unimportant offers

With a single mouse click You could be in the process of signing up for a monthly subscription to catalog. Even if it's just $20, you're spending money you had no desire to buy at all. There are also a few techniques that subscription companies employ like free subscriptions in the initial month for customers, but automatically debiting the credit card after the following month. Certain companies will even offer vouchers and other freebies to their customers to encourage customers to sign up. The best method to cut the cost of your subscription is to review your credit card statements as well as your email accounts. Be sure to not provide your personal information to anyone in survey or emails for promotions. If you discover that you're on some mailing lists you do not remember you can request the emailers to remove your name from the list.

Find articles written by business experts.

Many individuals find reading financial articles boring. If you find the ideal article for you, then you will know how to effectively save to invest. Successful investors who are successful with their investing strategies are also willing to share their stories, and it is available everywhere on the web! If you learn from their tips and strategies, you'll be able to get a the right direction for your type of investment. The advantage of listening to financial experts is that they can inform you of new ways to gain more profit. This is also that some people buy newspapers and go through the section on business. If they can find out what businesses are working on to achieve, they'll have an understanding of the areas they could invest their money, without having to risk their money with a shaky business. Read financial or business pieces may be to handle at first, but it's a great way to make your money more efficient.

Learn Time Management

When you invest, it is likely that you also put your time and energy into it. A majority of people think that investing isn't suitable for them since they aren't able to develop their investment, even though they have the money to invest. Experts consider time to be the greatest asset one can possess. It can be challenging to make the investment when you're an active person or you aren't aware of the tasks to prioritize. If you master time management and time management, you'll be able prioritize the work you need to accomplish within your day-to-day routine. You could also allocate an hour each day to develop your investment strategies and expand the amount of time later. To make the most of your time, you should determine the short and long-term priority investments. For example, for the short long-term goals, you're planning to create your own business in the span of 3 years. In the long run your company must be able to expand internationally. When you are managing your time, you're in charge of your objectives. This can aid you in reaching your goals since you'll are aware of the direction you're headed.

Money is a valuable instrument used by people to pay for their necessities. But, it's also the reason people are prone to falling from the heights of success. The people created money, however, money is the main force in the world. There are instances where money is the master of our lives, and it is not the case around. Remember that spending is not a problem however if the expenses result in debt perhaps you ought to think about what you can do to save in the near future. If you are in a position to develop good money habits, you'll be able to create a the capital needed to invest in your dream.

Chapter 5: Tips to guard yourself from fraud

when you invest

There is a belief that people with goodwill are not susceptible to fraud However, this isn't always the case. Every day , people with good intentions fall into the trap of fraud, as just goodwill isn't enough. People who come up with strategies to take people's funds are among the most brilliant minds around.

"There are some very clever and effective fraud schemes, so it is foolish to not be a victim"

How can you safeguard yourself? It's easy to take a few basic steps will allow you to avoid becoming the victim of fraud.

Secure your personal information

If someone steals your credit or checkbook and used it to purchase goods and if they steal you bank account information, they could be able request the checkbook and then write an account to your account. If they can obtain sufficient personal information to impersonate you, they could do so. This means they could withdraw money from your account at the bank and purchase items using credit cards, or obtain loans on your behalf. You could be in jail for a crime that you didn't do!

To ensure that you do not become a victim of this kind of fraud, make sure to secure all your personal documents including account statements from banks, your driver's licenses and ID cards. Don't share your financial or personal details with anyone else unless you have an underlying reason. This is especially true for credit card numbers and for your bank account. Don't reveal your debit or credit card numbers unless intend to purchase something.

It is possible that you won't believe it , but fraudsters search through trash bins for the information. So instead of throwing papers that include personal information in the trash It is advisable to destroy it up using a paper destruction machine. This is applicable to cancelled checks and bank statements, as well as Brokers information and driving licenses, credit cards and passports with expiration dates.

Use logic

Many scams are based on the promise of raking in huge profits. They generally aim to make investors draw others and earning an income. The same is true for other websites. certain websites request users to pay the first name on a list, and they give you the assurance that you will receive thousands of dollars if your name is on top of that list.

Think about the following scenario to clarify In the event that a project begins with five people and each convinces five others to join the program The number of investors increases to 25. If each of the 5 convinces the other 5 to join that they should join, the total number increases to the number of 125. If this process is able to reach the 9th stage, nearly 2 million people must be able to draw in over 9 million more! These types of program promoters are well aware of the fact that there's a level of saturation. Once this stage is attained the participants get the money and then run away. After that, you've lost your money and the person who you enticed demands that you to return the money they have lost.

Are you being offered simple cash or massive profits as a reward for investing? Beware: if it seems too good for it to be real, it's probably. Don't be enticed by any advertisement or anyone who claims that it's the most affordable deal on the market.

Have you ever received an email or phone call claiming that you have were the winner of a prize or a lotto? Beware of being very excited as this could be a scam which has been deceiving numerous people.

For instance one woman from England received an email from Canada informing her she had received the prize. The first step is to send $ 25 to cover the cost of the transaction. When she's paid after which she received a telephone message from Canada to inform that she had been awarded the third prize in the raffle worth $250,000, however she had to pay a specific portion of the prize in order to complete the transaction. and then she didn't receive any reward.

If you're being required to pay for an "free present" or prize, there is no doubt that you're being cheated. You should ask yourself: "How do I win an award in a game which I didn't participate in? !"

Do business only with people who are trustworthy.

Be careful! The scammers know how to earn the trust of other people. They are charming and skilled at what they do. Every seller, honest or even liars, are aware that they need to earn the trust of a buyer before selling to them.

However, this doesn't mean you should not be suspicious of anyone However, being vigilant is essential to safeguard yourself from scammers.

Don't trust your instincts to judge if the bidder is trustworthy Pay attention to these tips:

Does it seem like the offer is too tempting to be authentic?

Are bidders trying to convince you to accept the bid?

The Internet provides a myriad of offers that look too amazing to be real and offers a variety of valuable deals, however, it also gives scammers the chance to lure those who are caught in their web and not even knowing who they are.

If you're a user of an email account, it could be bombarded with a plethora of commercial and promotional offers. Even though these advertisements cover various items and services, the majority of them are bogus. If you're happy with one of the advertisements and you decide to pay to purchase an item or service it is possible that you will not receive the order or orders but not getting the value you paid for. It is best not to purchase anything you can't get from these advertisements. If you're looking to purchase something online, you should go to a reputable and well-known website.

This is also true for those who contact you to market the product. While many of these calls are legitimate businesses fraudulently marketing goods or services over the phone can cause businesses to lose billions of dollars every year.

The person who is scamming you could appear to work for a bank or credit card provider. If that occurs, then you should be suspicious of the individual who is calling to request your personal data since the information they want is what your company or bank should have a history of. To confirm if the individual calling is genuine and comes from the company or bank You can request his or her phone number and ask to call them back once you confirm that the phone number is from the company or bank.

It is advisable not to provide the credit card numbers or other information about yourself to anyone who calls you. If someone attempts to sell products or services that you are not interested in You can say politely: "Sorry but I don't purchase anything over the phone from anyone whom I do not know." If you do, then hang up. There is no reason to why you should speak to an individual you don't already know.

Chapter 6: What financial investment important for you?

Financial investments are a type of asset in which you put money in the expectation that it will grow or appreciate in value, which will allow you to draw a than you can imagine in cash. The concept is that you'll be capable of selling it at an even higher value in the future, or make money out of it while owning it. To build anything in the next few years like saving to buy a car, or in the next 30 years, such as planning your retirement plan, you might be interested in investing.

The way you use your money could be radically different. If you're considering a financial investment it is usually necessary to consider how long you have before making a choice. The longer you're able to wait, the higher risk you can be able to manage. The greater you're willing to take more, the better chance of making more cash! It is essential to emphasize that there is an economic understanding of investment which focuses on the way companies invest in goods machines, equipment, factories as well as personnel and inventory in order to manage their financials. This session is on financial meaning of "financial investments." Let's take a examine a few key concepts to know in relation to financial investment.

The amount that an investment appreciates in value is known as appreciation. For instance that if you purchase one share of stock for 10 dollars, and it's worth $15 one year later and the stock has increased by $5. Dividends are distributed on financial assets is usually performed in cash

Take control of your time. Time is the most valuable resource

Have you ever thought about the things you consider as your most important asset? Do you have a bank account that is overflowing? What about your health, relationships and your precious time? It appears that the last particularly isn't yet in the consciousness of everyone. Another way of looking at it is that most people undervalue the significance of time. However it is the only thing that is not able to be restored after it's gone.

The process of filling up an account that is empty and making new friends after old friendships come to an end is feasible. It is possible to regain your health after a sickness and restore your body through other methods. However the time element is unique in that once it's gone, it will never be recuperated. Additionally, as our existence is limited in comparison to other commodities and resources and resources, we need to be treating it with much more respect than been in previous times.

It is said that time is an all-encompassing commodity According to the saying.

In fact, Napoleon Bonaparte recognized this: "The only criminals that don't face punishment as a result of our system are the time thieves." In the event that you think about this you will have a great opportunity to increase your life's quality substantially. It is important to remember how good our lives isn't determined by our hourly rates or our salary, nor the worth of our stock investments in the longer in the long run. The only thing that really counts is the time that we've put into it wisely and with wonderful family and friends. The year you live in always has the same amount of days, weeks as well as hours, minutes and seconds like the year before:

Each year's calendar is split into 52 weeks, and each day is 365. There are 8760 hours and 525,600 minutes over the course of a year, or 31,536,000 second in all. If you're a billionaire or are living at the brink of poverty, the flow of time is constant. This is why the concept of time is seen as to be a universal benefit. That is it's not a matter of which person has the most time rather, making the most of what you do have.

Who is in the lead this time?

There are times when we feel like we are wasting time scrolling through Instagram since we're not asking ourselves a crucial concern: Who is in charge of this moment? It may be necessary to reconsider the priorities of your time if the answer is Instagram or an uninteresting Netflix show you don't like, or anything different.

Sometimes, the answer may need to be "my boss,"" "my kids," or "my taxes," depending on the circumstances. Find other strategies to make the response your personal, for instance, taking walking, or meditating or doing something that makes you feel happy. However, don't get too hard on yourself as well; it's acceptable to watch five seasons from The O.C. in a row , now and over and over.

It is important to track your time

In addition to small-scale business owners, every employee who works 9-5 has trouble in managing time. There are, however, many time tracking software available to aid you in solving this problem quickly and effectively. However, many haven't made advantage of these tools because they think that tracking time can be a waste precious time and resources.

Find out more about how you use your time.

How many times you've glanced at your clock and thought "Where was the day gone?" Fortunately, you are now able to provide a concise and concise answer to that long-standing question by tracking your time. If you keep track of your routine activities for at least a week it will be possible to determine when you're most productive , and the times you're just wasting your time with things like email, social media or just staring on the walls. When you cut down on the distractions and activities that are unnecessary and distractions, you can better manage your tasks, increase your productivity, and dedicate more time to your most important tasks. This helps you identify areas where you have to make changes.

When you start recording your time, then you'll be able identify the various areas in which you'll have to make some adjustments. Finding areas you require to improve goes beyond the reduction of time-wasters mentioned within this post.

Take the following example In the event that you're a graphic designer and finds that you're spending too much time with thumbnail logos, you can determine how much time you believe you should be spending in these types of logos. It could be that you're providing the customer with too many options. Try offering three or four options instead of 10, and making any necessary adjustments from there.

It aids you in billing correctly.

Or, do you prefer to be compensated per hourly rate for your expertise or by a fixed amount for your completed project? If you are charging by the hour, the client must know how many hours will be required to finish the project. If you charge per project, the client must be aware of how long it takes you to complete the project regardless of the fact that you charge per hour. Monitoring time spent on previous projects could aid in forming more precise estimates for future ones.

Remember that clients aren't thrilled with paying for work they believe could be completed faster. Time tracking software provides documentation that shows the amount of time you've spent working on a project with greater details than ever before. The client's concerns about the invoice are taken care of and time theft can be reduced since you charge the client in a proper mannerThere is no guesswork about the dates and times you didn't record and there's zero time loss.

It makes you focus on one task at a time.

It's been established that humans are incapable of multitasking in any way. In reality, the notion of multitasking is an invention. Instead of being able to manage multiple activities simultaneously you're alternating between them in a quick manner when you need to. This improves your efficiency and, in itself, is among the main reasons to monitor your time.

When you're tracking your time is completed, you're aware about the reality that every interval of time, whether it's fifteen minutes, or even an entire houris documented. This means that you need to be punctual in your work because you'd like to record it properly even if you're just spending a few minutes doing a variety of tasks, your journal will consist of a mess of entries. Being able to set aside some time for one topic that is crucial, in contrast is something to be admired.

It assists you in establishing the habit of behavior and routine.

If you are able to keep track of your time you can begin to establish routines and routines. This can eventually help you in fighting the urge to delay and allow you to maximize your resources. Habits and routines can assist you in maintaining a health active, joyful, and productive life. You can also boost your odds of becoming an effective "Unicorn" by doing these exercises.

It aids you in maintaining a healthy work-life balance.

It is essential for your own well-being and productivity as well as the overall health and performance of your family and your community to keep a healthy work/life balance. That is undoubtedly doubt one of the top reasons to monitor your time. It is essential for people to be involved in democratic life, family life and other community-based activities to achieve success. They also need time away from their work in order to refresh themselves and to build and keep friendships as well as their non-work identities.

When you've logged how much time was spent on your task, you'll see that you've gained extra time in your day. This is equivalent to more time to spend with family or friends members. The time you have is more to devote to things you truly enjoy.

If you can establish a healthy work-life balance, it's possible to stay healthy both physically and psychologically. This will help you in staying efficient and focused and will make you more likely to avoid burning out due to it.

Time can be the most precious of all items.

Within the realm of commodity it is time that is the most important. You've become such a valuable commodity that you are not able to buy more. It's impossible to retrieve once it is gone. Time is another thing which people tend to waste. When it comes to actual things (money or food, gold or silver, etc.) when we are unable to replace something, we might swap it out for something else and even gain more. It's difficult to recover the time lost that we've put in today.

Even the wealthiest man on earth, Jeff Bezos, would never be able to any up for the time he's wasted or invested. Time however isn't a discriminating factor. Both of us have the exact amount of time remaining and can't acquire more time in the near future.

Unfortunately, the majority of people live their lives without realizing that every day minutes, hours, or days is one less day, minute or hour to live their lives. They treat the time as an unlimited resource, like they were invincible.

The only method for you to "gain extra duration" is to focus on the most important things and be more efficient. Businesses who want to increase their profits only have two options: reduce costs or boost productivity. They have the option of growing their profits or cutting the cost of doing business.

There are also only two options to earn additional time for the things you must do in your day-to-day life. There are only two options.

* seek out innovative ways to boost your efficiency

Reduce the amount of time wasted. Since we are unable to create more time from scratch Our only choices are to:

Our resources are limited, and there's only the amount you can accomplish to increase productivity within a specific period of time. Eliminating time wastage is a lot more difficult than boosting one's levels of productivity.

The most efficient way to boost productivity is to not spending time.

One common misconception among the younger generations is that they are not able to have lots of free time. This belief is also which is also shared by many older folks too. We project our experiences and lives in the near future as we make a plan.

However, it does not take into account one of the most important aspects of the issue: as we get older, we're given greater responsibilities to manage and complete. This reduces how much time we are able to spend on achieving our goals. Most people spend their time doing insignificant aspects of their lives.

Many people continue to waste time in the name of "entertainment" and insisting that entertainment is crucial in their life. It's fine but only if you know where you're spending more time and choosing to dedicate more time to recreational activities.

As a rule, I try to combine my leisure time with something educational or useful. For instance reading a book, running for a walk or writing are all things I love to do to keep me busy. A method of productivity can help me make the most of the hours I spend and make the most use of my time and resources.

It would be completely different if we weren't working in a set time frame. You can accomplish everything when we allow ourselves enough time.

It is assumed that you are forever to prove our point. You are able to spend an unlimited amount of time to complete and research whatever you want to. You can become an expert in virtually every field, whether it be aerospace, science and philosophy, finance or another. The best ever chess player The most well-known musician and the most dazzling artist are all within reach for you to become.

Since you're blessed with unlimited amounts of time, you've been through a lot of years of experience to develop your skills in every area of expertise. This means that your inherent talent is diminished to the point that it's almost useless. It is the fact that we can have an inexhaustible amount of time more than compensates the lack of ability.

There are no excuses. Everyone has the identical amount of time to them.

The CEOs who have the highest stress levels and an overloaded schedule are aware that their time is their most valuable resource. It is clear in their heads that they don't have enough time during the day to accomplish all the things they must complete. Because of their time constraints it is imperative to arrange your life in the most efficient method feasible.

Successful people are able to effectively manage their time and ignore items that are not contributing to their goals. They're adept in saying no and avoiding engaging in activities which are not necessary.

Everyone around the world has the same amount of time as time doesn't differentiate between us and them. The absence of time should not be used as a reason to deny access. Presidents of the United States and top CEOs and executives get the same time that is available to them each day. Yet, they can accomplish much more during each hour of their lives. It is not a good idea to make the excuse that you don't have enough time to finish your task.

If you've ever had the feeling that you don't possess enough free time it's important to consider the reasons you believe that this is the situation. What are you doing in your spare time? What is hinders your ability to work? What is distracts you from your goals? The management of time is crucial when it comes to a task that is significant enough to you, you'll be able to find the time when the opportunity presents itself. When it comes to commodities time is most valuable commodity.

Affixing a price to your life

The length of your life is a limitation and no amount of money will make up for the loss of time in the world. The more aware we become that this is the case, and more crucial our life appears in our minds. It's your turn to acknowledge the value of this precious resource and take care of it. What's the most effective method of doing this? It's as simple as this: for all of the activities you do regularly and often, consider whether they're worth the time you dedicate to them. Do not waste your precious time in pursuits that don't bring you joy; instead give it to people and things that make you feel happy instead. This could range from a getaway to tasty food to hobbies. Only you who decides the things you want to trade you life experience for. Make an informed choice!

"Magic bench" or the so-called "magic bench."

We'd also like to share a short story of our own to you. Imagine the following scenario If you've won this prize in a contest: Every day the bank will deposit the sum of 86,400 euro in your checking account. But, there are two rules to this game. The first is that anything you don't spent before the end of your day is confiscated from you by authorities. The funds cannot be transferred to a different account, they are only available to spend the funds. Every day, when you get up you are greeted by the bank who opens an account under your name and an amount of 86,400 euro for the coming day.

The third rule is that the bank is able to end playing at any moment without notice. The bank can declare anytime "it has come to an end." It is a game that is coming to its conclusion." They also have the power to shut down your account and block the opening of a new one. What do you think about this scenario? Would you put your money on anything you'd like?

It's true that this game is actually a simulation of the real world. Each of us has the "magic banks." A lot of us are blind to the existence of it. If we get up in the early morning, we receive an extra 86,400 seconds to live for the entire day. That can be described as our "magical bank. Our time doesn't belong to us once we fall asleep in the night, since we are not able to the ability to access it. What we didn't feel the day has gone. Yesterday is gone. Every day the account is beginning to replenish itself with fresh cash. However, the bank reserves the power to close your account in any time and without notification.

What do you do with your 86.400 minutes of unproductive time every day? Their worth in dollars is a lot greater than that in euros? Be grateful and make the best usage of the time you have. Your life should be lived to the fullest because there is only one life to live.

Chapter 7: The Kinds of Index Funds

Since index funds are an increasing trend that is constantly changing, there are new kinds of index funds being released in the marketplace. The index funds that are being offered currently come from a variety of companies. Every investment in the categories of index funds has an expense ratio that is unique to them and a the minimum amount of initial investment.

Although this chapter won't contain all index funds available on the market but I'll try my best to offer you a variety in index fund. Of obviously, the selection of index funds will differ according to an individual's preferences. For instance, if I present you with a list of top index funds available certain investors may agree with the list, while others will not.

But, I will provide you with a list of some of the most inexpensive index funds that are available. After that, I will go over the is the best index fund to be aware of, which can be an additional individual preferences section. This chapter will conclude by addressing how to determine the right index fund for you. While I won't take long on this part because I'll continue to talk about how to choose the best index in the chapter 5. I will provide you with some brief information on what you should look for so that you can decide which index fund is best for your lifestyle.

It is among the Best Index Funds

If you are beginning to consider some of the most popular index funds out there You should consider what the return is in relation against your cost ratio. In other words, you'll want to get a return that is higher that your cost ratio. This is one reason that index funds have become sought-after. As you can see below cost-to-cost ratios are lower than the expected returns that index funds will earn.

Schwab U.S. Small-Cap ETF (SCHA) has an expense ratio of 0.06 percent or $6 for every $10,000 put in this index fund. The expected one-year return is 16.54 percent. If you are looking at a five-year expected return, you'll see approximately 12.39 percent.

Fidelity Total Stock Market Index (FSTMX) is a fund with expenses of around $9, or 0.09 percent for every $10,000 of capital. The expected return after one year is 14.71 percent, and for five years it's around 13.16 percent.

Vanguard High Dividend Yield ETF (VYM) has an expense ratio of 0.08 percent, or $8 per $10,000 invested. The one-year expected return of the index funds is 9.46 percent. In contrast to other index funds it is expected to earn a return over five years. is higher at 11.40 percent.

Vanguard S&P 500 ETF (VOO) expense ratio is 0.04 percent. The expected one-year return for the index funds is 14.52 percent and the five-year return yield coming in just lower at 13.45 percent.

Vanguard Total Stock Market Index (VTSMX) has an expense ratio of 0.14 percent, with an annual return of 14.71 percent, and a five-year return of 13.14 percent.

Cheap Index Funds

When it concerns index funds, investors generally prefer to choose the cheapest.

There are many reasons to this, including the limit on spending by investors however, many prefer to go with the least expensive funds due to the fact that every index fund does exactly the similar thing. This is why many people ask why they need to spend more money on expensive index fund when you could have the same results with less expensive index funds.

However, now that you have some of the top index funds is there a fund in that list that are among the most affordable index funds? If you're interested then explore the list below.

Vanguard Total Bond Index (VBMFX) and Northern Bond Index (NOBOX) are thought to be two of the most affordable index bond options on the market. Both have the same cost ratio of 0.15 percent per 10,000 you put into. However, they differ with respect to the amount that you must put into the bond. You must put at least $3,000 in the Vanguard Total Bond Index, however, you'll only have to invest $2,500 in the Northern Bond Index.

A lot of people prefer to buy index funds that fall under the category of small capital. This means the business is small. The investments that are made in these companies usually have greater benefits than larger corporations because their returns are increasing. Additionally they're typically priced lower. This means that you will not only earn a higher return as time passes, but are also investing less money investing in the fund. The two most affordable Small Capital Index funds that are available on the market are Scwhab Small Cap Index (SWSSX) and the Northern Small Cap Index (NSIDX).

Scwhab Small Cap Index Scwhab Small Cap Index has an expense ratio of 0.4 percent for every $1000 invested in the fund. Additionally it is worth noting that it is the Scwhab index is among the few that do not require a minimum amount of money. In contrast it is the Northern Small Cap Index fund must have at minimum $2,500. The expense ratio for the fund is $15 and that's 0.15 percent for every 10,000 dollars invested.

There are two index funds: the Vanguard High Dividend Yield Index (VHDYX) as well as Vanguard Value Index (VIVAX) Vanguard Value Index (VIVAX) are both well-known as high-value index funds. They are both considered to be the least expensive, indexes, with Vanguard High Dividend Yield Index having the Vanguard High Dividend Yield Index being able to offer an 0.15 percent expense ratio for each $10,000, and Vanguard Value Index with a cost ratio of 0.17% per every $10,000. Vanguard Value Index at 0.17 percent for every $10,000. Both index funds require a minimum of $3,000 for their initial investment.

In addition to this, it's worth noting that the Vanguard Growth Index (VIGRX) is ranked as the most affordable large index fund for growth. Its companion in this group can be found in the Fidelity the NASDAQ Composite Index (FNCMX). It is a Vanguard Growth Index requests a minimum investment of $3,000 and an expenses ratio of 0.17 percent. In contrast, the Fidelity The NASDAQ Composite Index comes with the highest expense ratio of 0.3 percent, or $30 for every $10,000 you invest , with no minimum investment requirement.

Since some of the most well-known index funds belong to the S&P 500, I will review the two most affordable investments made from this fund. The first one is that of the Schwab S&P 500 Index (SWPPX). This index fund has the expense rate of 0.02 percent, which equals $2 per $10,000 invested. It does not come with a minimum amount of this investment. The expense ratio and the minimum initial requirement are similar to those of the lowest S&P 500 index fund, which is Fidelity 500 Index (FXAIX).

What are the best funds to know About?

There are numerous index funds you need to be aware of. But, it's crucial to remember that just because these funds are the funds that many people suggest they should be aware of, doesn't mean that you should not investigate other kinds that are index-based funds. There are many index funds to purchase , but you must ensure you do your research to choose the ones that provide the highest returns and are appropriate for you.

The bottom line is that you need to select the right index that's not just varied but also inexpensive. Here is a list of the top indexes for stocks that meet the criteria.

Bond Index Funds to Check Out

There are many bond index funds that are believed to be popular in the current market.

Most investors will inform them that among the most effective ways to ensure your portfolio is varied is to include one of these bonds index funds.

The Aggregate Bond Index, often called"the BarCap Aggregate is among the biggest and most famous bond indexes on the market. It doesn't just include all the bonds that are on the United States market, but it also covers a variety of foreign bonds.

It is the Vanguard Total Bond Market Index (VBMFX) is widely known across the globe as being among the top bond index funds. It is among the only bond markets, if but not the one which gives you access to the entire bond market via its purchase. It has an expense rate of 0.16 percent, with a minimum amount of $3000 and is thought to be quite affordable considering the benefits it offers you. It's among the broadest bond indexes available, as it includes bonds from corporations small to medium-sized businesses, treasurybonds, longer-term and short-term bonds.

Vanguard Balanced Index Fund Vanguard Balanced Index Fund is exactly what its name suggests. The Vanguard Balanced Index Fund is known for its wide range of both bonds and stocks. It is thought to be among the most balanced index funds in the market. However the index fund is reputed to have one of the greatest advantages between its expenses and its returns.

Forever Index Fund Forever Index Fund

Warren Buffett has told people that the best choice for his portfolio is one will never need to be sold. That is Buffett's primary objective is to buy the index fund that he could keep for the rest of his life. Buffett also believes that all individuals should have this exact goal. In the minds of a lot of people, the most reliable index to keep for the long term can be found in it's the iShares Core S & P Total US Stock Market Index (iTOT).

One reason that investors believe the iTOT is an excellent investment to keep for the long run isn't just because the costs are minimal, and it's diversifiable in the field of index funds. This means that you're less likely to to be concerned about ensuring that your portfolio isn't contaminated by other investments since you find this kind of diversity with the iTOT. Additionally you will find that the iTOT provides excellent returns because of the low costs. The cost ratio currently is 0.03 percent, or $3 per $10,000 you put into the iTOT index fund.

Another advantage to this iTOT index funds is the fact that virtually every stock that is listed on the United States market is part of the index fund. This means you will not need to search for more time to find additional investments like you did when you bought the iTOT. Since this index contains so many stocks, it could result in an increased risk when purchasing the iTOT. But, as you're able to mix solid stocks, and less stable stocks and the index is capable of balancing itself between capital gains and losses.

Other Index Funds with Popularity

This fund Vanguard Growth Index (VIGRX) is referred to as an index fund that holds lots of capital stock, however, it also has those stocks that are experiencing the greatest growth within this group. Keep in mind that one of the main factors you should be aware of as an investor in an index fund is the magnitude of the projected growth you can expect from the investment you make. While this may mean higher risk, it offers more advantages over the long term when you look at it in comparison to other index funds that are popular that are available. In order to invest in this fund, you need to be able to make an initial minimum payment of $3000. The expense ratio is around 0.22 percent, which equals $22 as of the year the year 2019.

An additional Vanguard index fund that is currently very popular on marketplace is Vanguard Mid-Cap Index Fund (VIMSX). If you're purchasing Index funds classified as mid-cap, it is important to research them thoroughly and select funds that perform better than larger-cap index funds because they will provide you with the most favorable outlook. One of the biggest advantages of mid-cap and smaller-cap funds is that mid-caps have the least risk. While you will generally see more growth in smaller-cap indexes, you could enjoy the same level of growth from mid-cap indexes if you conduct your own study. It is important to determine what mid-cap indexes offer the highest returns when comparison to small-cap indexes. Many feel they are in the VIMSX index provides the best of all these benefits and is a mid-cap-investment.

It is the Schwab Total Stock Market Index Fund (SWTSX) is an index fund with approximately 70% of large capital stock within it. The fund has also witnessed gains on its yields over the course of a decade, which ranged from 10 percent to 12%, which is thought as high-quality in return growth for index funds. In addition it is worth noting that this fund SWTSX offers one of the best expense ratios in the market, with 0.05 percent.

The Fidelity Total Bond (FTBFX) is an index fund thought to be comparable with the Vanguard Total Bond Market Index Fund. The index fund comes with an investment start-up of $2,500 and a higher than the average expense ratio for index funds of 0.45 percent. But this does not mean you won't get a significant return or growth from this fund. Indeed, this fund has a wide range of high yield investments that are more likely to provide higher yields the longer you are this index. Additionally it's known to be a safe investment with low risks and is diversifying, which will give you security when you need to ensure the portfolio you choose to invest in is diverse.

It is the Wilshire 500 Index Investment Fund (WFIVX) is another well-known index that has a wide range of capital firms with large assets. The fund contains around 1,000-2,500 stocks, with more than 75% of them come from major capital firms. In addition, around 17% are medium capital companies , and smaller firms make around 8 percent. Additionally the top five largest holdings of Wilshire 500. Wilshire 500 index make up approximately 15 percent of total portion that the index holds. This is an extremely unusual percentage for shares of an index. Most of the businesses that make up Wilshire 500 Index are in the areas of technology, healthcare or financial. Wilshire 500 Index are in the technology, healthcare or financial sectors of the employment market. Although this Wilshire 500 Index is believed to be among the most reliable indexes available on the market, and a lot of users agree, you cannot enjoy all the benefits of it without paying an expensive cost ratio that is 0.63 percent for every $1000 you put into. While that may not seem to be a lot, if you look at it in comparison to other index funds with an average expense of around 0.05 percent and the Wilshire 500 Index can be a bit expensive.

Another well-known investment option that is available, and is an ETF is called the iShares Russel 3000. The ETF follows the index of the identical name. Around 12% of this fund's assets are made of the five top stocks on the index. In addition, the index includes a large number of capital firms, accounting for around 80 percent of the market. A lot of buyers are turning towards IShares Russel 3000 because of the yields investors have received over the past 10 year from this fund. In 2008, the fund's returns have been growing and is now offering an average of 12% in return. Additionally it doesn't have an excessive expense ratio, at a minimum not when compared to indexes like that of the Wilshire 500 Index. The Russel 3000 is an iShares Russel 3000's expense ratio is at around 0.2 percent.

How to Determine What Type Is Right for You

It's often an overwhelming task to figure out what index fund is the best for you, when there are numerous. The list above doesn't even begin to reveal the number of index funds available today. It is important to keep in mind that investors are continuously working to improve the quality of index funds available that are available. It is a more recent method investment in market, which means you'll see create new types of index funds as well as changes within the existing index funds. Of course, this will create more challenges particularly when you're just beginning your journey.

But, you don't need to search for the perfect index fund just for yourself. Actually, it's not something you would need to do especially in the beginning. You can not only conduct your own research, but you could get the help of your financial advisor or broker. Most importantly after you've got an understanding of the kind of investment you wish to concentrate on whether it's bonds, stocks or some other type, they will inform you which index fund to invest in. It will also allow you to gain a better understanding of what is right for yourself by conducting your own research which is the reason it's a good option to conduct your own study, even if you have hired an advisor or broker to assist you in your research.

It is also crucial to be aware that it's appropriate to start with a small amount. There is no need to ensure that your portfolio is stocked with diversification immediately. Although this is a possibility in index funds since the majority of indexes already have a diverse portfolio but it's not something you need to concentrate on right away. Instead, you could begin with a test run to see if you can find a good fit. You can select an index you believe will be most suitable for you (and your advisor or broker believes is best in your case) and concentrate on this fund to gain more about investing and the type of portfolio you'd like to create.

Unfortunately the investing world isn't as black and white as many might think. There aren't any strict rules or guidelines that provide you with the exact type of investment choices you need to make when you're building your portfolio. But, there is various tips investors have shared that they believe will aid you with getting started in your investment career. When you utilize the resources available for you, like advisors, brokers advice, tips, and research and tips, you'll be able to locate the top index funds for you.

Chapter 8: Setting your Financial Goal

After paying off your debts and building an emergency fund The next step is to determine the things you intend to make use of your funds to purchase. Allocation of resources is among of the fundamental issues that economics attempts to solve. This issue arises because there is a finite amount of resources as well as an innumerable list of needs and desires.

The best way to tackle this issue at an individual level is to determine the needs and desires you wish to prioritize most. It is possible to do this by studying the various possibilities you can invest your money, and then determining the ones you would like to invest in. Let's begin with the initial step:

Step 1: The process of identifying Future Goals and Expenses

The process of setting a financial goal begins with your plans. It is possible to begin by imagining the items you would like to purchase in the near future. The majority of us are already doing this. But only a small percentage actually contemplate their goals. The majority of people think about their dreams and hope that someday they'll be able to afford their goals.

In order to begin your own goals-setting process, you should make your list of items you'd like to purchase in the near future. Some of the items you might have on your list could be crucial, such as buying a house or establishing an investment fund for retirement. Other options, like having a long vacation or purchasing a sports car are not as essential, however they can make us feel happier.

After you've created your list, write an id next to every item, with 1 attributable to the top purpose. Here's a sample list you can use to base your own on

Make a Wedding Fund

Find a house that's large enough to accommodate the entire family

Save for the college of your children money

Save for dream travel destination

Certain goals come with a set timeframe. If you have children for example , and you're saving money for their college funds The fund must be in place when they finish high school.

Step 2: Choosing the Target Amount

If you are working towards those financial targets, you must take them on by one at a time. While we all want to meet all of the goals on our list, we're more likely to reach our goals quicker if we concentrate your financial resources on ones that are the most significant to us. When this particular target is achieved it is time to move on to next that is on our list.

Step 3: Organizing the Saving Timeline

Once you have your financial goals established choose the most important one , and create a timeline to save for the target. By tracing the timeline, you'll be able to determine what time frame you must save to reach your final goal.

In the previous chapter, it's recommended to make investments in stocks solely to achieve your long-term objectives to reduce the risk. Choose a financial goal that's some time away from being completed and set it as the objective of your investment activities in stocks.

Step 4: Evaluate the amount of improvement you will need to meet your objectives

The main principle of the investment process is that you require your savings to increase in order to achieve your financial goals quicker. It is important to make the right choices in regards to the potential growth of your investments. Certain trades could produce upwards of 15%, while other are likely to result in losses. It is more reasonable to anticipate a moderate rate of return between 7% and 10% per year. A few novices who make mistakes on the stock market might be able to enjoy lower returns on their first few years trading. Although these returns might seem small, they are higher than the majority of investments available.

If you know the average return on the market, you'll be able make an assumption about how long it will take your money to increase to the amount you want to reach. If you're sitting with $10,000 now , and you put it into a savings account and receive an average 8percent return every year that means it will take longer than 9 years to achieve a $2000 goal. You can increase the likelihood of hitting that goal by adding more money to your account each month. You can also boost rates of expansion by investing in stocks that have high growth rates in the initial trading period.

To understand the relation of the rate of return and the time needed to get there you can use a compounding interest calculator. For this kind of calculator, you'll be required to enter the capital amount and the time period in which you'll be investing for, as well as the annual rate of return that you anticipate to receive the amount you will receive. Any additional earnings that you earn from your market is reinvested into it, creating an exponential effect. This can help you achieve your goals quicker.

Fifth Step: Practice using paper Trading

If you believe stocks are the most suitable investment option to achieve your financial goals, you can boost your chances for success through practicing your trading. It is possible to begin with trades you make on paper.

It is possible to begin with a paper trade by using note in a notebook of the stocks you wish to put your money into. It is possible to begin by selecting among these options, and make an imitation trade, When you do your mock trade, select the stock and determine your purchase price as well as the amount of the purchase. Finally, you decide on the conditions that you'll sell the stock. In the coming months, days, or years, you may begin to monitor the stocks you chose to evaluate the results of your trading mock.

It is possible to make your mock trade more real-world by setting a budget like the one you'll need in the event that you begin trading. This will stop you from becoming reckless with your selection of stocks.

This kind of mock trades let you to test the strategies you use to trade. If your mock trades are often result in losses, you might need to change how you approach trading.

Paper trades allow you to be more familiar with the market as well as the various events happening at the moment before even stepping foot with the marketplace. This lets you test what it would be as if you invested in businesses that you think to be within your area of expertise.

The most important thing to do with paper trading is to practice it as often that you are able to. This will let you be aware of which indices, sectors and companies have the highest returns.

Step 6: Get Started

If you are aware of what you'd like to accomplish and how you will accomplish it, you can begin making progress towards your financial goals. You can start by saving money for an investment fund. Request your broker for the minimum amount you'll require to start investing. While you're saving, begin to research the companies you'll purchase with your initial investment. This will help you ensure that you'll be ready to begin investing after your savings have reached the minimal investment amount you need.

Chapter 9: Conversion of currency

When you begin Forex trading, it is essential to understand what it takes to change currencies, and also to notice the difference in their values as well as the way the exchange rates of currencies differ across international lines. This means that you will need to be aware of not just the currency trends and values of the local market, as well as those of foreign markets.

Working in several currencies

Of course, as Forex is a foreign exchange market, it is not possible to expect everyone to buy or sell dollars or euros (and why would you not would you be asking? However, keep in mind that not everyone wants to trade in these currency types). With all the variables and currencies that are volatile in the market, how do you identify the right purchase or sale when you spot one without knowing the worth of the currency?

It is the first thing to locate the source that gives you an overview of the exchange rate currently in effect between your currency of choice and the currency of your choice. It is recommended to create an overview of each currency you're dealing with. Of course, it will not be precise to the centimeter or even a fraction of a particular currency over the course of a whole day, but you'll have a starting base from which to begin similar to north on the compasses. These sources are available everywhere on the Internet and in many brokerages on the internet and in person.

Conversion of currencies

It is important to know how the currency conversion is described. The exchange is usually done using a ratio referred to as"cross rate. In this case both currencies are listed as an XXX/YY ratio with the XXX location being known as being the basis currency. It is typically represented as an in number and the YYY position expressed as a decimal value that is closest to the base currency's rate. It's similar to the term "miles per gallon" or the number of revolutions per minute in automobiles - a clear comparison of one to other by the ratio.

The smallest amount or decimal at which the currency is traded is known as a pip and it is the amount at which a cross rate can be expressed. For instance, if British sterling pound is traded in thousands ofths, the currency is expressed in 3 decimal places. It is the US dollar is typically expressed in the hundredth of one cent (the fourth decimal place).

In the case for an exchange ratio the value of one U.S. dollar may be equivalent approximately 117.456 Japanese yen. The ratio is expressed as 1.000/117.456. Base currency nearly always expressed as one unit (e.g. one dollar, as opposed to 10 dollars) typically, the measurement will be that of the U.S. dollar. Because the number (or huge number, as it's known) of the currency secondary to it in the YYY spot changes very rarely in terms of conversion typically only the decimal portion of this number will be used on the foreign exchange market.

So, you might see in the above ratio that the yen's value is at .456 without mention of the 117 total of yen that is shown in the ratio. This is due to the fact that the exchange rate may differ between 117.456 to 117.423 however, it is not able to reach 119.024.

A change in the major number - all the way up to and prior to the decimal mark - could be far too significant change in value for just a few trading days and is an extremely rare occasion that could trigger the market to shift drastically either way or the other, unless it was that the number was within just a few thousandths.

The most commonly used currencies that are used in forex trading include the US dollar and the British sterling pound and the euro, as well as the Japanese yen as well as the Australian dollar. The past was when there were other currencies worth keeping in mind (such like the Franc and the Lira as well as the German mark). But, since the consolidation of the majority of European markets trading in Forex in the Euro several currencies were made obsolete, which made trading on Forex easier for different countries.

If you purchase a good in a particular currency and the value of the currency is lower than dollar value, such as the U.S. dollar, you could earn money selling the same item in dollars. It is the same vice to the other side if the value of a foreign currency rises over that of the US dollar. Of course, you'll only benefit from this scenario if the product is sold in two currencies and both markets. We'll discuss this procedure in future chapters, along with other ways to make the most of the market for foreign exchange (such the arbitrage) and in greater detail in the coming chapters.

When you have identified an basis for a specific currency, and the rate at which it converts against other currencies that are traded on Forex You will be able to track the rate of change in the rate of conversion as well as its fluctuations and the volatility. These ideas won't appear "foreign" to youand you'll be on the same level as the pros and will know the ropes.

In the wake of this learning You must then master the ability to comprehend, read and comprehend and then interpret market developments.

Trending in Forex

Charts, following the advice of chartists and market analysts and learning how to make informed predictions on your own can help you keep track of different marketing trends.

In the next chapter, you'll be taught more about the use of statistical data to predict the next trend in the market. Are you going to have a clean and calm day with no movement, or is there the forecast for a storm that is brewing, with the rumblings of uncertainty and change? What can you predict about what's likely to affect your stock the next day, or in the foreseeablelikely future?

Understanding and interpreting market patterns in a meaningful manner can help eliminate common fears and anxieties for novice traders. In reality, the most effective way to starting out in markets is look up the news on it or the sections on finance in the newspaper which outline the patterns and the expected results. In the next section, you'll be able to be taught how to interpret the data and fundamental trends.

Chapter 10: Mutual Fund Categories/Asset Class

There are many categories or asset classes that are available for investment. Here are some of them:

Government Bonds

Corporate Bonds

Municipal Bonds

Balanced Funds

Stock Funds

International Funds

Global Funds

Sector Funds

As you can imagine, you could spend a significant amount of time talking about every category in detail, but I'll provide a basic diagram for you to refer to. You are able to discuss these categories more in depth in your meeting with the financial adviser as well as the 401 (k) reps.

Government Bonds are bonds made from government of the United States Government. The principal benefit of this fund is the lower risk of defaultbecause the bonds included in the portfolio are insured by the complete credit and faith that is the U.S. government.

Corporate Bonds are bonds that are issued by Corporations. They typically have an increase in yield over government bonds, but they aren't secured with Governments like the U.S. government.

Municipal Bonds Municipal Bonds: Bonds issued by an authority of a state, county town, city, or state authority to fund projects. The interest earned on these bonds are not subject to federal taxation and, in certain cases, could be exempt from local or state taxes.

Balanced Funds They is a mutual fund that has invested bonds and stocks in their fund. The proportion of bonds and stocks can differ in each fund. For instance, a balanced fund could contain 60 percent bonds and stocks. A different fund might contain 65% bonds and 35 percent stocks. The risk risk is determined by the ratio of bonds and stocks and their risk exposure to the market.

Stock Funds They is a mutual fund that invests in stocks. It is crucial to know the investment strategy of each fund and its goals. This is where you'll need to find out whether the money manager is investing in Large Cap or Mid Cap and Small Cap stocks. Also do you know if the manager is investing in stocks for growth or value, or is it mixing (blend)?

International Funds They can be mutual funds which invest in stocks that are not based in the United States. With the global economy, there are many big companies that operate all over the world. These kinds of funds give exposure to these businesses.

Global Funds: These funds invest in U.S. companies and international companies.

Sector Funds: These funds focus on certain sectors that are in the market. For instance, you could buy a fund that concentrates on the Energy sector or the Healthcare Care sector. The money manager buys bonds or stocks that are within the fund's primary sector.

They are concentrated and are not diversifiable.

Once you've got an overview of various asset classes that you can invest in, we'll look into the differences to understand the distinctions between Large Cap, Mid Cap as well as Small Cap mutual funds. There are also differences between bond funds. However I'll concentrate more on stock funds.

Large Cap Mutual Funds are mutual funds which put money into Large Cap sized companies. They are businesses with an estimated market capitalization of more 10 billion dollars. Let's return to this Vanguard Equity Income Fund. You're likely to recognize the names that are in their top 10 holdings. These are large businesses which exist for quite a time. In the 3 categories mentioned above, the Large Cap stocks are considered as more stable than smaller-cap firms. They have a large amount of outstanding shares and an abundance of private or institutional buyers.

Mid Cap Mutual Funds are mutual funds which are invested in Mid Cap sized companies. These are companies that have an estimated market value of between $2 billion to $10 billion. If you look at the portfolio of of these funds you might recognize certain companies but you may not identify the names of the other companies. Middle Cap mutual funds usually believed to have a more aggressive strategy for investing in comparison to large Cap mutual funds.

Small Cap Mutual Funds are mutual funds which put money into Small Cap sized companies. They are businesses with an estimated market value of less that $2 billion. You are unlikely to recognize those names for these firms. The Small Cap mutual funds are usually thought of as an aggressive way of investing. Small Cap stocks offer greater growth potential, but they do not have the capabilities that larger Cap stocks. They also are more susceptible to events or news that are negative.

Diversification and Asset Allocation

Diversification and Asset Allocation are crucial when investing. This method of investing gives you exposure to a broad range of industries locally as well as internationally, across various types of assets. By diversifying your investment portfolio, reduces your risk of being exposed to problems that can arise within a specific industry. However, this doesn't mean that your investments are safe from the general market volatility.

Let's look at this more. Asset allocation doesn't mean that your investments are diversifiable. In other words, you might be investing in an Small Cap domestic mutual fund or an Mid Cap global mutual fund as well as an Large Cap international mutual fund. When you review the holdings of mutual funds and you will see that the three mutual funds all have an incredibly high proportion of investments in the technology sector. Although you've made investments in various categories of investments, you're not diversifying your investment portfolio.

Diversification involves investing in various industries and the different asset classes. Here's a great illustration of how a portfolio that is diversified could appear.

We've covered bond and stock funds in a previous chapter. The REITs include Real Estate Investment Trusts and Precious Metals are items like gold. As you can see, this portfolio includes five distinct asset classes. Each asset class changes according to their market. The portfolio isn't confined on one market, thus the risk is spread over a variety of markets.

Let's return to our mutual fund instance The Vanguard Equity Income Fund. It will be apparent that the money manager purchasing their investment across 11 different industries. But, if you take a closer look, you'll be able to see that the manager is investing 40% of fund's capital into three sectors: Financial (17.2%), Healthcare (17%) as well as Consumer Staples (12.79%). This information is crucial as you start looking for other kinds of mutual funds you have and how they are allocated.

It is essential when discussing your investment portfolio in conjunction with your advisor to financials or 401(k) agents to have the full picture of your allocation to assets and diversification. As I stated earlier that just because your investments appear to be spread over a variety of types of mutual funds, it does not suggest that you've got the variety you want.

Chapter 11: Should I Be A SWING TRADER?

Do you wish to participate in the stock market, but feel it's just too difficult for you? Maybe you have working full-time at work and don't have the time to be sitting at your computer using a direct-access system with your your mouse, waiting to click. You require a style of trading that doesn't force you to be bound by your investments and waiting at the end of the day. What you must consider is the option of trading swing stocks that are suited to your needs and yet allow for the same joy that traders gets from making excellent trades.

Swing trading is a varied style that is popular because of numerous reasons. It is based on strong downtrends or uptrends which allow traders to move on a trend for as long as it continues. The traders who use swing trading base their trading choices on a large amount of research that they conduct in the midst of working and other responsibilities. Therefore, trading stocks in swings offers the flexibility needed to be able to trade stocks. Research is required to gain a better comprehension of what stocks you are keen to and investing in.

The research that needs to be conducted will look back on previous trends, allowing you to make an informed choice about what you should do. So you will be able to calculate the risk on what the duration of the trend in an upward trend or how long you have to be in the downtrend to make the most of the profits. The use of charting at the end of the day software and the data supplied by your broker can also be used to assist you in making the decisions you make regarding your stock trading. This means that you do not need direct-access systems, which means you are not tied to your stocks , and waiting for the close of trading.

Most swing traders typically deal in block sizes of 1,000 shares at a time , however it is more of a reference point than an absolute rule. Additionally, they are able to hold only 10 positions at any one time. The types of stocks the swing trader would choose to pick for their stocks are ones that are able to be traded rapidly or at least in the near-term future. Below is a list of the factors employed by the trader to study the stock and choose the images of the stock.

Volume and Liquidity

If they are looking to buy stocks, they will swiftly move when they deal with active traded and large stocks that are simple to trade.

Current

This is the downtrend and uptrend mentioned earlier. Stocks that follow these patterns of trend rather than a straight line is what traders on swings are searching for.

Volatility

A stock's volatility is evidence that it has lots of movements. Another indicator that a trader will look for is the fact that traders could make money quickly from the volatility of a stock.

Sector Selection

If shares are trading in the high sector, the swing trader will find trading easier, however in the weak sector , the profits are earned by trading short on a stock or declining price.

Tight Spreads

Tight spreads are characterized by small spreads in bids and request of a stock. Swing traders prefer the narrower spread since they will make more money from it. A wider spread means that the trader is likely to make less profit. The tighter, the spread, the better.

Swing trading stocks are an alternative method of trading that is suitable for those who have an active job but still would like to trade. It requires lots of work, however it's more flexible to conduct trading. Just make sure you take the time to complete the necessary research to find the best swing trading stocks and you'll be able to feel the excitement that other traders experience after a successful trade.

THE TRILL OF SWING TRADING

Swing trading is in essence an aspect of stock trading. However, the skills required is different from usual techniques. A disciplined approach to daily happenings of every market is vital to be a skilled swing trader, as it's not something we are able to test to see if we are in the right place, as we are investing actual money into it.

If you're not confident of taking risks, then swing trading isn't the best alternative for you. There is no doubt that low-risk, low-reward trading is a very secure method. However, in swing trading that has higher risk, you may reap a good profit. The first decision that an investor in swing trading should make is the time to begin and when to exit the market in order to earn a profits. To make this decision, they don't have an exact or precise approach.

Swing trading is comprised mostly of two actions: purchasing and selling bonds, options, stocks and commodities, currencies, etc. But the process is becoming complicated when you consider when to purchase and sell these items. Swing traders aren't able to determine the optimal time to earn a high return on investment by using accurate timings for buying and selling. The objective should be to purchase at low prices and sell at timings of the highest prices.

The swing trading industry is heavily dependent on the maturing market's behaviour. Swing traders earn profit or loss due to the good or incorrect decisions made by other companies. If you are able to profit from the incorrect timings of other traders you could make a huge profits by executing in the right way. However, you must be willing to sit and wait for the correct timings without having to rush some choices. Sometimes, however, a lot of speed will be required to make the most of the circumstance.

Making the right decision in the correct time is vital. Swing trading isn't about moving in a herd. The loss of one person is the gain of another. Thus, self-discipline and patience as well as the capacity to analyze are key aspects in this. Try to maximize the profit while minimizing the loss to the portfolio.

Another thing to note about this type of trading could begin buying at the beginning in a stock that is trending, and keeping it. At the end of this trend, the stock will be traded. Thus, trading happens mostly based on changes in the trend. The duration of this strategy could be anywhere from a week to the duration of a month. It is entirely dependent on the direction of the market of the individual swing traders. The knowledge gained will assist traders who trade swings to establish their timings more clearly and with precision. This will in all likelihood be an extremely short-term process.

Since planning is crucial when it comes to swing trading, traders typically seek out the guidance of the past history of businesses before entering into agreements. Since this is a short time period, the selling and buying of stock must be swift. In this regard, investors who trade in swings will favor stocks from the most heavily traded well-known companies on the market. This will allow the process of entering and leaving more quickly. The buyers will buy at the start of the growth phase of the specific stock, and then attempt to sell it before it returns to lower levels.

Before you begin swing trading, you must be sure of your abilities, and you will have the most out of trading stocks. This will help you gain lots from the strategies for swing trading. Plan your strategy and execute the right thing by focusing on your trading on the stock market.

SWING TIPS FOR TRADDING

Swing trading is among the trade styles that are typically used in speculative activities on financial markets, including bonds, commodities foreign exchange, stocks and index of stocks. The majority of the time, this style of trading calls for a trader to keep their trading position for more than one trading day, typically between 2 and 5 trading days. The popularity of swing trading in trading because the style of trading generally offers a high risk and reward ratio. This means that the chance of earning profit is greater then the chance that could increase with each trade.

In general, the swing trade is aimed at a 100-pips profits with a high probability. The potential for profit can be realized from every market shift. The trader who is a swing, particularly on the stock and foreign exchange index markets, is able to trade either short or long to make the most of every opportunity. Also, during an entire trading week, when the market is in a volatile state and a trader is in a position to encounter a variety of trading opportunities that he or she could take advantage of.

As compared to scalping and day trading it is evident that swing trading offers fewer trading possibilities, however, as you will see when you adopt this type of trading, you'll be able to spend more time on your other things since you don't have to be watching an exchange all day. Of course, you'll not have as many opportunities, however you will have a high chance to win every chance. It is your choice to decide which style of trading to use. The best trading styles are not perfect There is always a plus and plus and.

If you do are interested in giving a shot at swing trading you could discover some strategies using the many websites. There are books as well as other informational materials about swing trading. You could also go to and become part of certain trading forums, too. But the problem is that there are also a few fraudulent individuals who claim to be expert in swing trading but they're just asking customers to buy their useless educational materials. Be wary of these individuals.

If you can gain basic knowledge and experience in the swing trade, you will be a successful swing trader too. You could create your own strategies for swing trading. Many individuals enjoy the benefits of creating their own swing trading strategies because they're the sole ones to understand their trading personality needs, style and. Do not stop trying how to become a successful swing trader. Although without doubt, it takes longer to master the art of swing trading however, in the end all your efforts will be worth it.

COMPARATIVE ANALYSIS ABOUT DAY TRADING and SWING TRADING

Stock Market

The stock market that shares owned by companies can be traded and purchased. The primary purpose of an exchange is to gather capital from investors through the sale of the rights to own (i.e. shares) and in return, businesses give dividends on each share. Investors are the ultimate owners of the company, therefore, the amount of shares indicates the strength of the shareholder. With time the concept of frequent ownership change of shares has been observed which results in capital gain or loss. The share, in turn is a source of dividends and also capital loss or gain. Therefore, a stock market has two kinds of investors that are investors and speculators. The investor is primarily concerned with dividends, while speculators focus mostly at capital gains or losses. A person who invests starts with fundamentals while the one who speculates begins with the technical aspects. A prudent investor takes decisions with a sense of realism while speculators exploit the market's emotions. It is fascinating to observe that capital gains and dividends or loss show fluctuations and trends. A speculator or investor takes a chance because of the uncertainty of patterns and fluctuations; as a result they reap the advantages or lose. Simply put, the stock market can transfer risky investments from investors who are not willing to take on risk to those that are prepared to take on risk when they are compensated for it. It is a way of risk sharing to help the company's development. Additionally, when shareholders research the company's technical aspects and the fundamentals, they is educated about Organizational Behavior (OB) that is exhibited by the business. Research efforts enhance the shareholder's business acumen and is a positive learning impact of the market. An experienced worker should reap some financial benefits from share business.

Trend Phenomena in Stock Market

The universe we live in is multifaceted. Every aspect of our cosmic economy whether inanimate or animated, is a constant part, varied segments as well as repetitive content. It also has evolution features, which means that it displays an predictable pattern of pattern of behavior. For instance seasons are not a constant and follow a certain pattern; in addition, they repeat. Based on the available information about the seasons, an accurate forecast of seasonal behavior is possible statistically. Human behavior is characterized by certain personality traits due to natural-born abilities and instincts. The main abilities are perceptual emotional intelligences, execution intelligences. While the primary instincts include parents' instincts, gregarious instinct or learning instinct, as well as sexual impulse. The presence or absence of some intelligence/instinct content shapes countless human mindsets/behaviors such as fear, greed, haste, panic, love, hate, speculation and prudence. The behavior of the economy, e.g., demand of something, is a result of multiple perceptions and emotions. The economic behavior, like buying and selling of shares can be measured quantitatively through the movement of price and volume. The technical analysis therefore is built on the Revealed Preferences, i.e., actual sales and purchases of shares. In economics, the word "trend" is a reference to the steady fluctuation of prices. When it comes to share market trends volume is a part of price actions. The dissociation of chaos from the trend of volume and price is the main focus of the technical analysis. A better understanding of trends provides competitive advantage to traders, both investors and the speculator.

A trend generally has three periods of duration, i.e., short-term medium-term, long-term and short-term. Typically, traders view the duration of a trend that ranges from few days to a couple of weeks as a short-term-trend. lengths that range from a couple of weeks to several months are considered to be medium-term, and longer durations are known as a long-term trends.

The term market of bull (up) or the bear (down) market typically refer to cyclical losses or gains between 15 and 20 percent or more.

The cycle of market cycles that are up or down typically lasts from a few months up to a few years. In the 10-20-year timeframe stock market cycles have multiple bear and bull markets. These long-term cycles are known as "secular" markets. There are bear and bull markets.

When a trend alters its direction, it's known as the turning point in trend. A turning point is determined on the behavior of sellers and buyers that are both dynamic and static which means that it can reveal certain predictable characteristics. Technically, turns indicate the prices of resistance or support. The prices of support or resistance are indicators of the existence of static elements of a collective mind and the shift in the level of resistance or support is due to the dynamic nature of the collective human self. The static behaviour of economic agents forms the an essential element of static economic analysis. However, the changing behavior of economic agents reveals that they are dynamism, and calls for an analysis that is dynamic to gain a complete understanding of the economic behaviour. Thus, static-comparative and dynamic analysis is utilized to determine the changing economic variables. The most commonly used statistical tools to analyze are average as well as standard deviation and correlation.

Benefits of the Trend Phenomena

According to the saying, trends are good friends. While the market is awash with long-term trends that investors can discern daily, monthly or weekly trends. Profits are generated every hour and a skilled trader who can understand, and know more and grow, will be able to benefit from these trends. Certain short-term trends indicate the beginning of larger-scale movements on the markets. Investors/speculators who find these looming possibilities can profit before everyone else figures out that a trend has begun.

A share is intrinsic and market value. In the end, intrinsic value for an investment is determined by business fundamentals, while its market value is determined by the demand and supply conditions of the share at a specific point in time. In the long-term both the value intrinsically and the market value of a share are in sync with each other, however, there is a difference between the values intrinsically and value in the short and medium time frames. A smart investor/speculator who is wise takes advantage of the possibility of divergence of prices and reaps the benefits or capital gain from investments.

The exit and entry are two distinct elements of trading in stocks. The entry of a trader's trader is the departure of a trader. The risk-return strategy of the opposite traders results in a real trade. The decision to enter is more an art rather than science and is based on ongoing trading activity, market sentiments , and the individual risk-return analysis. The management of your portfolio and exiting in contrast is primarily scientific rather that an art. The real profit or loss will be the deciding factor when it comes to closing.

CHAPTER 12: 7 Top Real Estate Investing Jobs

Real estate investing has been proven for a long time that it requires a lot of CAdollars for active investors. A lot of the strategies and methods to purchase real estate to generate one of the biggest (and the fastest) CA$H are based on an amount of patience and facts (i.e., Little Capital and no credit!) to be able to cash out a massive cash-flow quickly!

This is one of the reasons to take real estate investing classes for the majority of citizens. make offers that require very little or no money however, you will reap huge benefits from your expertise and time.

In the majority part of "Real Estate' investments, there is no investment however, for certain periods there is no ROI other than the time-for-money component.

This is why I call these types of jobs"real estate investments" they stop earning money when you quit working.

Real Estate Investments in these professions will never give you financial independence, while earning you cash because they bring in quick cash and do not provide long-term, deferred income.

One of the most difficult issues to overcome is you think about buying a property the cost of the acquisition is far higher than what you would expect from a normal job. Many people aren't prepared for the discussions.

I'm sure that when you were a child you believed the $X figure was huge thing, but then you realized it was only one hundred dollars or perhaps even a few thousand dollars.

However, when it comes to buying real estate there are also the thousands of dollars.

The majority of people don't really care about these numbers and don't earn the amount they ought to.

They didn't even know what Real Estate Investment vocabulary.

One of the most important lessons I give my students is to overcome the fear of having to learn about the hundreds of thousands of dollars and alter the programs given to them as they were children to develop flexible thoughts about money and take part in earning even more.

A simple step to begin this process is to look within yourself and consider how much money you're feeling. Can you talk about numbers of several hundred thousand dollars with ease?

Most people can learn quickly, with bit of practice.

In this manner it's the right time to take a close glance at these real estate investment specialists.

These "jobs" provide different revenue rates according to the location We'll be looking at them by a percentage viewpoint instead of discussing these in dollar terms.

The amount of time, energy, and time you invested in it will yield much (or less) by using these examples.

1. Property profiling is a popular method of gaining access to real estate investing can bring an income that is decent to the real estate investor similar to of what factory workers perform in the region.

2. Leasing Purchas - this efficient device is a great way to purchase and sell property without cash (a sandwich) and still have a nice bag of cash (can you believe with me that it's an absolute favourite of my?) On average, those who work earns 1.5 to 3 times more than the property profiler.

3. Subject To-You could help this real estate investing strategy work well with a little preparation. When you are able to make these deals work that you can make your investment in real estate will be much lower for corporate executives.

4. While foreclosures can be extremely lucrative and are among the top ways to generate revenue from the purchase of properties However, the time and the resources required to complete these transactions efficiently are becoming extremely difficult.

The benefits of the people who make the purchase are enormous-almost 10 times more than profilers, however, the number of people looking for them is harder to track down.

5. Tax Lien Certificates- This is a real-estate investment, which is actually investing your money in something that will yield a profit. It is one of the most secure investments that yield the potential to earn more than the same level as any other passive investment.

If you have cash to spend this is the perfect location to start with the smallest risk of 15 percent or more return.

It's still a good investment to invest in real estate since taxes liability certificate are short-term and quick-turn profits generators, and don't last very long. Additionally, they require expertise and a certain amount of talent to increase their profits.

6. Short selling, a type of investing in real estate is a different challenge due to the degree of expertise and resources is crucial. Any kind of real estate investment that works as far or even more than any other type-will earn plenty of money if you have the expertise is there.

7. Equity positions and secondary bills - higher levels in real estate investments in which more information is required to manage the risk, however, returns on equity securities can

be quite impressive - ranging from 6-9 percent in the case of complete active results. There is no limit' with equity securities purchase.

Once you've completed the fake internal programming - the LIES that you've learned throughout your life about the importance of wealth beginning an excellent career in real estate investingthrough a myriad of investments in real estate and finally, a full-time real estate investing.

Five essential features that make Real Estate Investing Profitable

Every now and again those who are trying to determine the best place to spend their money, I ask whether real estate firms are more or more profitable than other companies in the area.

My answer is usually that along with its ability to make gains immediately Immobilizing can also provide long-term advantages.

Five benefits are discussed in the following paragraphs:

1. When you purchase a stock you hold it for a certain amount of time before selling it at a

profits. You can also refurbish real property (to boost it's value). The success of your stock is contingent on the management and performance of your business which is outside your control.

Contrary to traditional instruments of investment, such as those whose turnover rates for instance, are dependent upon third-party sources (e.g. the management of the business) Real property is completely in the hands of the control of.

Although you won't be able to observe demographic and economic trends or the consequences of natural trends but there are other factors you can control to increase the returns on your investment.

The examples cover the construction of improvements or renovations to the property and the occupants of it.

If you're doing it correctly the value of your investment will increase and increase the amount of money you earn.

2. When done right If done correctly, real estate investment has profitable even in the midst of a recession (like the one we're in

right now) It has been utilized numerous times to help avert financial crisis like those experienced by many people during the current economic downturn in Nigeria currently.

Many of my clients trust me and say that they're not conscious of the lucrative ways to invest their money due to the current economic conditions. Certain of them own bond and treasury bills that require new investments.

We had lengthy discussions and I recommended that landed investment be the most reliable and stable alternative investment route from my experiences in my role as a property agent.

This is because, even if every business fails however, the land will be highly valued. Then, I came up with the following quote from an former US President to help drive my argument to the heart of my argument: "The real estate can't be taken away or lost If it is handled with care It's the most desirable estate that exists in this country,"-Franklin Roosevelt.

It's not surprising that the customer was adamant and signed up. It was the logical choice!

3. So, by putting your capital in a productive immovable property can shield you from the devastating impact inflation can have on traditional investments.

The reason for this is that the significance of immobilization is typically diminished as a result of inflationary pressures. This is the reason why the prices of land and property rise when inflation increases.

The land's design gives owners the benefit of the ability to alter their prices in order to keep pace with inflation.

Rents for the month, for example could be raised to accommodate inflation, providing protection against damage caused by certain transactions in the financial market.

4. The Uniqueness of Being Widely Acceptable to be collateral The Securing Fund of Banks Today The property is the most widely accepted and accepts the kind of collateral that is used in Nigeria as well as other regions of the world, be it in the form of land or

buildings that have title to property (i.e. Certificate of Occupancy - also known by the name of "C of O").

It offers the benefit of being able to defend the interests of the bank and the creditor, i.e., after thorough review, the funds are granted and the terms of reference are accepted.

This is among the main advantages that of a privately owned C of O has relative to the global C of O because the earlier C (i.e. privately owned C of O) is the type of C that is typically used in financing transactions within Nigeria by the borrower who is aiming to get it.

5. The investment in real estate helps other people to make money. Also, even if you're not in a position to invest a lot but you can still invest. All you need is the know-how.

This is because the real estate market is considered to be a tangible item or a physical possession. This property's tangible nature draws in financial institutions, i.e., to buyers.

Therefore, real estate products are typically purchased with loans, unlike traditional investment products such as inventory that is not quantifiable and are therefore considered to be more risky to invest in.

Immobilien savings can be able to be achieved through money or mortgage financing. In the second case the transfer can be made to make it easier for you to pay or a trusted third party for small amounts.

These the payments are made to the land, which will continue to increase in value over and throughout the period of the payments. This gives confidence to the fact that the investment is secure to those financing the purchase.

It's not a surprise that real estate investments have enjoyed such a long time of growth!

lease Option Real Estate Investment Benefits and Drawbacks

A novel approach to start investing in real estate is to use the rental tool. The primary advantage of leasing options for real estate investing is that they are regulated. The developer has the legal right to manage and profit from an investment property without purchasing the property.

The contract of a real-estate lease is an amalgamation of two documents.

The renting portion of the deal will let the owner rent their property , while you pay them for a specific duration of time. The property owner isn't able to raise rent or lease the property to any other person or let the property go to any other person during the lease term.

The option portion of the contract relates to the option you purchased for the purpose of purchasing the home at some specific amount in the near future. If you wish to exercise your purchase right, the seller will then sell the property to you at the price agreed upon. The right-side of the contract obligates the seller to offer you the item during the period of option, however it does not permit you to purchase. The only obligation is to pay the rent according to the agreement during your rental time.

In the event that the lease contract option is properly written and designed correctly it will offer the lender with substantial benefits and benefits. When a "right for sub-lease" is provided in the option of the contract it will result in positive cash flow through renting the property to an individual who is a loanee for the period and then selling the property to a rental vendor to generate an increase in cashflow and earnings. If the leasing option is the term "right of assignment" the owner is able to transfer the lease contract to gain a quick benefit to a buyer.

The option of leasing for real estate investments is a secure high-leverage, low-risk investment option that requires almost no capital.

High Leverage - It's high leverage because you are able to take control of and make money from your property now, even in the absence of it. Losing control of the property often limits your financial obligation and moral obligations. It is only possible to acquire right to the land when you wish to purchase the property using this "right to buy."

A little or no amount of money The cost of the owner for the introduction of a lease arrangement with owner will require very little or no cash from his pocket because between the owner and the developer it's completely negotiable. There is also a range of ways that the fee can be set. It can be set up as a schedule payment or balloon payment, or any other arrangement that is mutually beneficial between both parties. The price of the alternative could also be $1.00.

In order to protect the properties to be sold in the future the owners of rental properties typically offer the seller an incentive fee that is non-refundable, which can be approximately 2% to 5 percent of the sales price they agree to. Based on the way in the way that the rental option agreement can be drawn out and put together and negotiated, the landlord could request an incentive fee paid by the leaseholder to pay any outstanding payments towards the lending institution.

The flexible real property investment contracts are an incredibly flexible form of ownership since the conditions of the contract, including the payment rate, days of pay and penalties and interest rate charges ballon charges, selling prices and many other clauses which are agreed between the investor and the agent. Both parties' obligations can be negotiated. For instance, if the owner is not willing to be the property manager, they could be stipulated within the lease agreement option that the rent owner is responsible for any minor maintenance and repairs.

Risk-free, financially - There is a low risk of financial loss because you are able to decide to change your mind, and allow the "option to buy" expire when the property doesn't yield enough interest to earn profits. If the tenant does not want to buy the property, you've gained from the tenant's optimism about their monthly cash flow as well as an additional, non-refundable incentive fee.

Check out an illustration of lease that could be purchased in a way that the buyer earns a profit through three different stages of the deal.

Profit #1: Non-refundable fee The future sales price that can be that is negotiated with the present owners of the business is $125,000 plus 2 percent that sales amount is an optional fee. Option Fee: at least $2,500 to the owners. The projected selling price for the tenant-buyer you have chosen is $155,000 and the fee for option is 4percent of the sale price. The fee for option you owe to the tenant-buyer is $6200. You get from the lease buyer $6,200. You pay the lender $2,500 and your earnings = $3,700 2. Net cash flow from leasing. The annual rental cost you paid to the owner would be $1,000. The lease rent you set for your renter at $1250 per month. You receive $1.250 from the seller of your rental each month and pay your landlord $1.000 each month. The rental period is $250 per month negative cash flow.

2. Profits: These are derived in the lease option contract when it is initially written. Third profit: The difference between your owner's bargained purchase price as well as your tenant-buyer's prospective purchase cost. Let's suppose that the home is worth minimum $155,000. Your client wants to utilize their right to buy. You buy the home at $125,000 from the landlord and then lease it for $155,000 to the tenant buyer. $155,000- the $125,000 you pay to the lender equals a refund of $30,000.

The key to leasing option is, obviously finding interested buyers and sellers. It shouldn't be a problem to locate these enthusiastic buyers and sellers. The continuous shift in the market for immobilization has led to a massive number of sellers being unable to sell their homes and buyers being unable to obtain financing. Sellers may receive an acceptable offer that can be paid in the near future, through the lease option to sell the property to an investor. The potential tenant-buyer could acquire ownership without the traditional home loan conditions that must be met.

A disadvantage of the rental option for investment in property could be the fact that the renter, or buyer of the tenant may not pay the monthly rent. The buyer will be able to be able to take the owner directly from the bank and proceed with the eviction process. But, there are some rules that can be inserted to stop buyers from failing in their payments. There is as well as a variety of clauses in contracts that could be added to an agreement for lease options.

If the owner fails to conduct due diligence before signing the lease option agreement the result could be with a property that is unmarketable. There could be a myriad of ties, concerns about property possession or forfeiture. If you take care when signing a lease option agreement it is possible for the lender to avoid the pitfalls. The lender can perform some things like conduct the background check and checks of credit on both the buyer and seller as well as look for information from the public in relation to ownership and property status, or look up the names.

Despite the few disadvantages, leasing is an excellent option to purchase immovable properties with minimal or no capital investment and minimal cost of financing. It's also a fantastic option to own an unowned property, create cash flow and possibly future income in a flexible manner.

The greater the amount of money you make in today's real estate business and the more you are able to appreciate and implement new strategies for investing in real estate and the greater gains you'll make in the current real estate market. Don't put off getting the knowledge you require to be able to invest in real estate to make it in today's market.

Innovative property methods and ideas to lease immovable assets, condemnation and wholesale.

How do you arrange every deal in a way that you get better results with each deal, and reduce the risk.

What should be included in your land contract now? This will allow you to avoid problems which could result in thousands of dollars!

The most crucial legal clauses you can include in every deal to eliminate any risk completely.

A step-by-step guide for investing in real estate with low risk.

Where and how to effectively examine the property efficiently and cut down on time.

The best ways to finance your investment property in a creative way.

How do I know the true value of the asset such that you don't overpay?

How to manage your assets with no checking on property or income, such as credit or property to allow you to accomplish more.

Chapter 13: Evictions

Evictions of tenants are something the majority of landlords would prefer not to deal without, but they are forced to deal with. Nobody wants to be involved in the arduous task of evicting tenants, no matter the reason. However, from time the time, any property manager will have to evict the tenants who have been causing trouble. No matter if you are against evictions or you are a fan of the mess it's important to fulfill your responsibilities legally. Every tenant is protected by the law, however, also the owners of property. In short the law doesn't function in a specific way. While you have to believe that the tenant has fulfilled their obligation but you have to also adhere to the agreement.

This chapter we're going to examine the emotive topic of evictions thoroughly. We will explore the circumstances in which you are permitted to expel your tenants as well as the obligations you need to meet prior to conducting an eviction. We will also consider the best method to conduct an eviction in order to avoid legal complications in the future.

Understanding the laws of your state regarding Evictions

The most important thing to keep in mind is that laws regarding eviction differ from state to state. If you live in one place, you might be permitted to evict your tenant at short notice , while in another state, an expulsion is considered to be inexpensive. To avoid legal problems regarding your tenant, be sure you've got a good knowledge of the state laws and local authority law. In the majority of cases the regulations governing the eviction procedure must be outlined in the lease.

Although you might be able to set different terms for eviction in comparison to those provided by the state authorities The lease agreement could be considered to be invalid in the legal court. Most of the time the rules contained in the lease will be deemed to be valid if they are in line with the guidelines that are set by local or state authorities. If, however, the lease contract contains regulations that contradict local laws, the lease could be deemed invalid. For example, in New York, the landlord is required to give an eviction notice that is at least 30 days prior to the date of expulsion. When the tenant been in the property for less than one year the 30-day notice would be sufficient. If the tenant has been within the residence for more than one year, but less than two years the sixty-day notice is required. When the tenant resided in the apartment for more than 90 consecutive days, then a written notice of minimum 90 days is required.

But, some landlords create their own rules and have tenants leave the premises within 30 days, regardless of whether they have resided for 5 or a year. years. If this is the scenario, your lease is only in force for as long as the tenant is removed within 30 days regardless of the length of their tenancy. If the tenant decides to contest the eviction before a judge, the lease agreement could be declared invalid.

Things to do prior to Making an Eviction Notice

The delay or disagreement with rent can make it necessary to submit an eviction order. While it's fine to file an eviction notice but there are some aspects to think about before getting going. This includes:

Know the laws governing eviction

Before you begin thinking about filing an evictioncase, make sure you know the laws governing the eviction process in your state. It is best to speak with an attorney regarding the procedure. The attorney will give you details of laws say about expulsions. A clear understanding of the legal procedure can help you come to your mind on what is considered to be the best decision to take.

Try to think of a rationale for your tenants

Before filing an eviction notice, you should try talking to your tenant. Engaging with your tenants can solve the majority of problems that result in an expulsion. If your tenant is in rent arrears, it is possible to negotiate a reasonable payment arrangement. The tenant is able to stay and you can get the money!

As we'll see in the future, keeping your tenants over the long run will lower your operation expenses. It istherefore essential to work to a mutual understanding with your tenant prior to taking action to evict them. If you choose to settle out of court which does not require an eviction, ensure that it's in writing. In this way, you will be sure to know about the eviction procedure in the event the tenant is in breach of your contract.

Find a reason that is valid to expel the tenant.

It is essential to establish a valid reason to file an expulsion notice. There are instances that you might want to request that a tenant leave your home, but you do not have a good justification. In this situation you could be caught in legal disputes between you and your tenant. If you don't have sufficient grounds and the proper proof for the eviction, do not attempt to file an expulsion. It is best to contact your tenant and request them to respectfully leave the property.

Collect evidence

If you're seeking to evict a tenant based on the conduct of the tenant, it is crucial to gather evidence. A majority of tenants appear in court with well-planned evidenceand ready to fight the expulsion. If the tenant caused damage be sure to document these damages prior to filing an notice of eviction. If the tenant isn't paying rent on time, be sure you have all the documents to prove the delay in the rent payment.

Do You Need to Involve an Attorney or Do You?

A lawyer can be useful in the event that you need to submit a formal complaint to an administrative court. In this case you must have the option of representing yourself in court or have the assistance of an attorney. You are not able to have representation from the property's manager or agent. In addition, the lawyer will assist you in understanding the laws that govern expulsions and ways to avoid expensive dispute.

What to do when you want to evict your tenant The Correct Way

If you are evicting your tenant you must follow the correct method to follow that is based on the lease agreement as well as the law. If you don't follow the procedure, you could not be successful in removing the tenant out of your home. However the tenant could cause more problems when he goes to court, requiring you to pay unexpected costs. Here's a step-by step guide to getting your tenants out.

Step 1. Have a conversation regarding your tenant.

Before you begin the process of eviction, you should talk with your tenants about getting the issue resolved. Your tenant should be made know that if he or she fails to make rent payments, you could be forced to issue an Eviction Notice. If you can come to the best way to settle the matter, it's better to resolve the issue prior to the filing of an expulsion.

Step 2: Create the notice of eviction.

If your dialogue doesn't produce the desired outcomes You can proceed and prepare an eviction notice. There are some who do the wrong thing by advising tenants via the word of mouth. Whatever distance the tenant is to you, notices of eviction should be written. Avoid using electronic mail or message. Make sure you send a formal letter and make sure it's delivered directly to your tenant. When drafting the eviction notice it is possible to make use of a template issued by the government or create your own template.

The notice of eviction should contain three kinds of details:

It is important to state the reason of the eviction.

When was the date for the expulsion and

A step that could be undertaken by the tenant in order to stop the eviction process. For example the tenant could be required to pay the rent due by a specific date in order to avoid being evicted.

Step 3: Give an email to the tenant.

After you've created an eviction letter that outlines the reasons for eviction as well as the date of the expulsion, take the time to deliver the notice in person to the landlord. It is typical to hang the notice at your tenant's door. In this way tenants will not have a reason to believe that they not received the notice. It is also recommended to deliver a copy via mail and then get an acknowledgement that proves the notice was delivered. You can also send a soft copy of the notice via the mail or via phone messages to make sure tenants receive the notice.

Step 4: Inform the court.

When you serve the notice of eviction to the tenant, you must be patient. The time period specified in the notice of eviction to expire before filing an action in court. The court will then schedule an appearance and issue the notice of the tenant for you.

Before you submit the case before the judge, you have to discuss the matter with your lawyer. You'll learn the possible problems which could impact the case. If, for instance, the case isn't financially viable, your lawyer will assist you in finding an alternative to making a court filing. In addition, if the situation is complicated, your attorney will be able to take more time to plan and file a case the most effective way.

In order to present your case before the court, you'll be required to carry numerous documents, which include:

Copy of notice to evict

The lease contract must be accompanied by a copy.

The proof of payment

Checks that bounce

The records of your communications and the tenant

Show that the tenant read the notice to evict

When you submit all documents The court will then schedule the date for the hearing. Both you and the defendant must be present at the hearing. But, you can also request that your lawyer attend for you.

Step 5: Finish the expulsion.

If you've done it all correct or as per the law, the judge is likely to rule to your advantage. The tenant will be removed from your property. If the tenant remains dissatisfied following the ruling, law enforcement officials will assist in forcing the tenant to leave.

Although some tenants might be stubborn and create a lot of issues in the process of eviction It is your best interest to stick to the procedure. Do not force your tenant away or lock their doors, or attack them. When you use violence in a manner that is not in the interest of the law enforcement agency or the court your tenant can make use of your actions against you in the courtroom.

Can you evict a tenant without a Rental/Lease agreement?

Lease agreements (signed by all parties) stipulates the circumstances in the tenant's rights to be expelled. If there is no written agreement that you must at the very least be able to sign an agreement in writing. Although oral agreements are not legal in the courtroom however, you could face to prove that your agreement is legitimate. In this case you are defending your word against that from the person who is defending. You might even be required to call witnesses to support your claim.

However, it is possible to expel tenants even if there isn't a lease agreement. Most of the time the absence of a lease agreement signifies that your property let on a month-to-month basis. Thus, the tenant has to pay rent on the monthly basis, in case of non-payment, to which you're allowed to initiate the eviction procedure.

In a nutshell, here's the things you should be aware of:

All expulsions must be executed according to the laws of the state and local authorities.

Before you file an eviction notice It is important to know the laws governing evictions. confirm the reason for the eviction and then gather evidence.

Although it is not mandatory however, it is essential to engage an attorney during an official eviction case, when the case must be handled in an civil court.

The process of eviction could be complicated if there isn't a lease agreement.

Don't take the eviction issue to your own.

Conclusion

You are able to be in charge of your finances, regardless of how different you may feel. If you're not knowledgeable about the concepts of money, interest, investing or stocks, you're likely to be able to control your finances and take control over your money instead of relying on someone other than yourself to earn any money. There is no one born knowing about spending money. Certain people are born wealthy while others are poor. While this can be a significant factor in determining the amount of money however it's not always an indicator of the level of understanding you'll have about the importance of money in your life.

If you can save money, you could build your own investment portfolio. It's only a couple of dollars per week to open saving accounts and, once you've got enough money that you can invest in, it may be able to get twice or even more of your initial investment. There's plenty to be done between investing your initial money and evaluating returns however, you must be aware that everything starts by savings to begin with.

The process begins by consolidating and removing the unnecessary expenses. Everybody has at the very least one expense that they could eliminate from their lives. For some, they can save hundreds of dollars every week by being clever with their money, and others may find that they've done all they can cut back on unnecessary faff. No matter what circumstance you're in, keep in mind that there's always room to save money.

Aiming to save ten percent of your earnings is a great method to ensure that you are prepared for retirement. You may need spend more that ten percent depending on your income at present and the way you plan to live in retirement, but you need to make sure that you're trying to save at least $10 per $100 you earn so that you can have funds to invest in your future.

Making a commitment to yourself may seem intimidating, but it's an excellent way to earn additional cash. When you only work for yourself and invest only in yourself, you will have complete control of your finances and make sure that you are responsible for making profits.

Concentration and studying will be your key to ensure that you're achieving success in your chosen field. Don't stop reading books on investing and stay informed of the most recent news regarding international and regional economics.

A strong belief system and a passion for what you do are crucial to ensure that you will make the best choices with your money. If you aren't confident in yourself and aren't enthused about the venture you've made money into, you'll never achieve true happiness or even success in your money-related ventures.

It can be an obstacle however it is essential to ensure that you're investing your money in a responsible manner. There are a lot of laws in place to safeguard your personal funds as well as the money of other people. There are also so many rules that are not explicitly stated in the game. Occasionally, you may have to learn things in the wrong way. The better prepared you are prior to making investing, the better likelihood that you'll come out with the top prize at the final.

It is crucial to ensure you're aware of common investment mistakes to ensure that you do not make mistakes by yourself. There will be moments where you regret your actions or instances where which you wish you'd had things differently. Be aware however that it's better to learn from others' mistakes to avoid making the same mistakes. need to repeat them on your own.

The mindset you have is essential to ensure that you're making right investment decisions. All the money you can make will not be able to protect you from your own fate if you do not believe in your capabilities as well as the items you're investing your money into.

The fear of failure will be the most significant hurdle. It's what will keep you in making the best choice and is the reason you fall to the edge of making the wrong choice for your finances or you.

The process of stepping away from your comfort zone will not be straightforward, but it's your only chance to be sure you're creating the change you want to see. You can't continue to do the same thing we've always done, and expect to receive the results we want to see that could be different.

Your risk level differs from that of anyone else's risk. While it's beneficial to study the strategies of other investors to figure out what you should not do, you must to keep in mind that your own risk level is likely differ from anyone other person's.

A long-term perspective is crucial to identify to ensure that you don't mess over the long run. The purpose of investing is to look towards the future, therefore we must ensure that we're preparing ourselves for success in the future, and not putting all the focus on what's most important in the moment.

Try to think in a simple way instead of too complex way. Certain things will require you to think and think more deeply however, you're also going to experience moments when it is crucial to look at things in a straightforward, rational sense. Listen to your intuition and to your brain. Anything else can make the process more difficult and lead you to make a wrong choice because you thought too much about things.

Be happy with the process Be happy, or you're likely to end up unhappy later on. If you are working too hard and concentrate too much about your investment and profits that you're making this is likely create stressand not achieve the satisfaction you wanted at all. Keep in mind that there is an explanation for why you've decided to invest. Don't keep anything else from stopping you from reaching your goals.

Start early, but make sure to begin small. This is your money, therefore you're not going to want to plunge into the deep end immediately. Instead, take a few steps before diving , so you are sure that you're not putting yourself in situations that are more difficult to get out of.

The importance of compound interest is to make sure you don't make any losses. These are the two main aspects you'll need to keep an eye on when you make investments in your future.

Diversification is one method for risk control. The more you diversify your funds and the greater security net is there to protect your fall if it happens. Take a look at all the choices when choosing which investment avenues to take. Real estate is a fantastic option for investing that seems to be growing more sought-after.

www.ingramcontent.com/pod-product-compliance
Lightning Source LLC
Chambersburg PA
CBHW050023130526
44590CB00042B/1823